Faithful Economics

Faithful Economics
The Moral Worlds of a Neutral Science

Editors
James W. Henderson
John L. Pisciotta

Baylor University Press
Waco, Texas

Cover Design by David Alcorn

Library of Congress Cataloging-in-Publication Data

Faithful economics : the moral worlds of a neutral science / editors, James W. Henderson, John Pisciotta.

p. cm.

Includes bibliographical references.

ISBN 1-932792-22-8 (pbk. : alk. paper)

1. Economics--Religious aspects--Christianity--Congresses. I. Henderson, James W. II. Pisciotta, John (John Lee)

BR115.E3F35 2006

261.8'5--dc22

2005032545

Printed in the United States of America on acid-free paper

To the 150 scholars who participated in the 2002 Conference on Christianity and Economics at Baylor University.

Be outrageous.

JWH
JLP

Table of Contents

Preface

Scholars from across the United States and around the world gathered for three days in November 2002 to examine the influence of Christian ideals and principles on economic thought. Conferees came from ten different countries and represented a diverse group of scholars not only in economics, but also theology, sociology, law, history, philosophy, and political science.

Funding for the conference "Christianity and Economics: Integrating Faith and Learning in Economic Scholarship" came from two sources. The plenary program, comprised of seven presentations, came from the Pruit Memorial Symposium. The concurrent sessions were organized as the Lilly Fellows Program Second National Research Conference.

With the secularization of U.S. higher education during the last half-century, institutional support has diminished for the integration of faith and learning in mainstream scholarship. Within this new social context, how should Christian economists and related academics with a faith perspective envision their academic discipline, approach their research, and guide their public advocacy?

This book addresses the challenges and opportunities facing Christian economists in the discipline today. As you read, keep in mind that this book and others like it are not the final word on integrating Christian thought in economics, but only an important interlude in the journey of discovering how Christian scholars can better address the economic issues facing them and better determine their Christian responsibility in this important task. It is our goal that your reading will both inspire your thoughts and encourage your scholarship as you consider this important topic.

We gratefully acknowledge the gift of Ella and Lev Prichard that established the Pruit Symposium as a permanent feature of the academic calendar at Baylor University. In addition, we thank the Lilly Fellows Program for sponsoring the Second National Research Conference that was an integral part of our original conference. Finally, thanks to over 100 participants and presenters who attended the 2002 conference.

Finally, we are encouraged by the growing interest in Christian scholarship in general and its application to the field of economics specifically. In addition to this collection, twelve papers presented at the conference were published in separate special issues of *The Journal of Markets and Morality* (2003) and *Faith and Economics* (2003). And we are aware of several papers that have been accepted for publication in economics journals that are considered more mainstream (North & Gwin, 2004).

With the secularization of U.S. higher education during the twentieth century, scholars of all faiths are challenged by an educational system that trivializes religious belief. Within this new context, academe encourages personal religious beliefs and at the same time considers it inappropriate to relate those beliefs to academic work. Thus, it is critical for scholars with a faith perspective to understand that either their faith is important and practical in their scholarship or it is irrelevant to their scholarship. This collection of papers speaks to the practical relevance of the Christian faith. We trust that these efforts will encourage other Christian economists in their attempts to make the Christian faith relevant to economic scholarship.

Introduction

The Christian Perspective and Economic Scholarship

James W. Henderson

With the secularization of U.S. higher education during the twentieth century, scholars of all faiths are challenged by an educational system that trivializes and even ignores religious belief. Within this new context, academe may accept personal religious beliefs but considers it inappropriate to relate those beliefs to academic work. Thus, it is critical for scholars with a faith perspective to understand that either their faith is important and practical in their scholarship or it is irrelevant to their scholarship.

Most scholarship devoted to the integration of Christian values and economics has been out of the mainstream, as defined by publication in leading journals and major university presses. While the basis of modern economics is functional atheism, a Christian perspective is not wholly absent. Such publications as *Christian Scholars Review*, *Faith and Economics*, *The Review of Social Economy*, and *The Journal of Markets and Morality* have shouldered the responsibility of promoting Christian scholarship in this arena. These publications assert that the Christian perspective should make a difference in the work and scholarly activities of economists. If the Christian perspective is not incorporated into the work of economists, its absence will likely create a vacuum where other worldviews will dominate.

The early twentieth-century economic writers spoke to the place of values and ethics in economic discourse (Stamp, 1939; Weber, 1930; Schumpeter, 1942). More recently, Kenneth Boulding (1968) and Nobel laureate Kenneth

Arrow (1983) addressed ethical issues outside the normal purview of economics. But as the Chicago School of economics ascended in prominence, the discipline became increasingly secularized, limiting the discussion of ethics, religion, and almost everything value related. As a result, late twentieth-century Christian economists have labored, for the most part, outside of the mainstream. That is not to imply that their contributions have been insignificant—but that they have had only a tangential impact on the profession as a whole.

This collection of papers speaks to the practical relevance of the Christian faith. The editors trust that these efforts will encourage other Christian economists in their attempts to make the Christian faith relevant to economic scholarship. The goal is to explore with Christian scholars from a variety of disciplines the appropriate ways of integrating faith and scholarship in economics. I believe that those interested in economics will gain insight from the seven scholars who contributed to this volume—two philosophers, one theologian, and four economists. This book is not meant to be a direct challenge of the neoclassical paradigm of rational choice, but simply the initiation of an important scholarly dialogue to integrate basic Christian values into the economic way of thinking. There is no single Christian viewpoint presented in this book. The authors do share, however, a common belief that scholarship shaped by Christian commitments is entirely appropriate and should be an integral part of the academic lives of Christian economists.

As you read, keep in mind this book is not the final word on integrating Christian thought in economics, but only an important interlude in the journey of discovering how Christians can better address the economic issues facing them as Christian scholars and determine their Christian responsibility in addressing economic issues. The editors hope that the readings will both inspire Christians and encourage their scholarship to continue to address this important issue.

THE DOMINANT ECONOMIC TRADITION

Advocate and critic alike agree that the assumption of rational behavior plays a major role in modern economics. Historically, rational behavior has used "self-interest maximization" as the primary motivator of human behavior. Some would argue that any motivation other than self-interest maximization is irrational—a complete rejection of any role for ethics or morals in decision making. As economics has become more quantified, in many ways the discipline has become narrower in its scope. Striving for precision, economists advocate strict adherence to the scientific method and its logical, value-free approach to research questions.

Perhaps the most notable economist endorsing the view that economics is value free is Nobel laureate Milton Friedman. Friedman (1953) argued that economics as a positive science is concerned exclusively with the factual and predictive. As such, it is independent of any particular value position or normative judgment. Positive economics is an objective science, in the same sense that the physical sciences and engineering are objective.

Normative economics, on the other hand, is more subjective in nature, dealing with issues related to ethics and values. The dominant view is that the two categories are independent, or at least that positive economics is independent of normative economics. In contrast, Friedman (1953) agreed that positive economics is independent of normative economics, but argued that normative economics cannot be independent of positive economics. Policy conclusions, by their very nature, rest on prediction based on positive economics: "Any policy conclusion necessarily rests on a prediction about the consequences of doing one thing rather than another, a prediction that must be based—implicitly or explicitly—on positive economics." (p.4)

The traditional positive–normative dichotomy is actually one distinguishing between individualism and utilitarianism—exclusively self-interested behavior, on the one hand, and an overriding concern for all mankind, on the other. Most human action, however, is undertaken somewhere between complete isolation and interaction with everyone else. Human action takes place within groups such as family, friends, neighbors, fraternal organizations, or members of the local church, synagogue, or mosque. Many actions are motivated by narrow self-interest, but many are not. Frequently, Adam Smith's famous quote in *The Wealth of Nations* (1937) is mistakenly used to argue that self-interest is all that matters:

> It is not from the benevolence of the butcher, the brewer, or the baker, that we expect our dinner, but from their regard to their own interest. We address ourselves, not to their humanity but to their self-love, and never talk to them of our necessities but of their advantages. (p. 14)

But Smith also spoke to mutual advantage in trade, and later in *The Theory of Moral Sentiments* (1975); he pointed out the importance of rules of conduct:

> Those general rules of conduct, when they have been fixed in our mind by habitual reflection, are of great use in correcting misrepresentation of self-love concerning what is fit and proper to be done in our particular situation. (p. 160)

People do not behave in an exclusively self-interested way. Nobel laureate Amartya Sen (1987) contends that people are influenced by a plurality of motives, pursuing goals other than self interest—especially in those circumstances where they are acting as an agent for another. He goes on to argue that

> The wide use of the extremely narrow assumption of self-interested behavior . . . has seriously limited the scope of predictive economics. . . . [And that] the jettisoning of all motivations and valuations other than the extremely narrow one of self-interest is hard to justify on grounds of predictive usefulness, and it also seems to have rather dubious empirical support. To stick to that narrow path does not seem a very good way of going about our business. (p. 79)

If actual behavior is not influenced by moral–ethical considerations, then economists expend an inordinate amount of effort studying questions dealing with issues such as equity, income distribution, discrimination, and access to health care. Thus, for all of economists' posturing, the inescapable truth is that economics is not value free. In fact, Fritz Machlup (1969) argued that it is impossible to be a good economist without knowing something about ethical values—if nothing else, to appreciate the objectives of policy makers.

It is ironic that the 2002 Nobel Prize in Economic Science was shared by two individuals who questioned the extreme view of rational behavior as the basis for economic decision-making. Daniel Kahneman, a psychologist, was awarded the prize primarily for a paper he coauthored with Amos Tversky (1979), where he questioned the way economists think about the theory of decision making. The other winner that year, Vernon L. Smith (2000), received the award for recognizing, through his use of laboratory experiments, that the predictions of the theory of rational behavior were not always supported.

SETTING THE TONE

How should Christian economists and related academics with a faith perspective envision their academic discipline, approach their research, and guide their public advocacy? Failure to integrate a Christian worldview into economic scholarship will convey the false message that the Christian perspective and its presuppositions have no place in the real world. Yet, there are serious questions about whether and to what extent the content of faith is relevant to the practices of the academic disciplines.

The 2002 Christianity and Economics Conference at Baylor University sought to contribute to the fulfillment of the hope expressed by George M. Marsden in his book *The Outrageous Idea of Christian Scholarship* (1997). As a result, it was obvious to the conference planners that the ideal person to deliver the keynote address for the conference would be George Marsden. The chair of the history department at Notre Dame, Marsden encourages Christian scholars that they do not labor in vain.

> It is time to recognize that scholars and institutions who take the intellectual dimensions of their faith seriously can be responsible and creative participants in the highest levels of academic discourse. . . . There are good prospects that the twenty-first century academia will be more open to perspectives that go beyond the Enlightenment on questions of religious faith. (p. 111)

To revive and establish scholarship influenced by Christianity, Christians must first recognize their current condition in the academy. This situation—even in church-related colleges, according to Marsden—is one of marginalization of the religion professed on Sundays. Steven L. Carter, in his book *Culture of Disbelief* (1993), gives a slightly different twist to the situation by referring to it as "a trivialization of religion." References to religion may be acceptable only when offered with no significant relevance for people's lives. Relating Christians' current cultural condition to the academy, Marsden offered these words in his keynote address: "Many professors who are firm believers in a traditional religious faith would never dream of trying to relate that faith to something so important as their scholarship."

While Marsden accepts that there are good reasons why Christianity has lost its position of dominance in American universities, academe has also experienced an "overcorrection." Why should Christianity be excluded from the academy? Christian economists should not accept efforts by their colleagues to block them out. More importantly, Christian economists should end their self-imposed ban from participation in scholarship as Christians.

Other "ideologies, outlooks, or social locations" have their places at the table of academic scholarship, including feminist, Marxist, neoconservative, gay, libertarian, and postmodern perspectives. Regaining Christians' scholarly footing can involve several dimensions, including taking into account the influence of background beliefs as Christians, selection of an agenda for research, and strategies for interpretation of research.

In all of these ways, Christianity is relevant for scholarship. Indeed, various "Christianities" are relevant. Clearly there is no single Christian perspective that will inform scholarship in economics or any other discipline. Marsden gives examples of the ways that Augustinian, Calvinist, Kuyperian, and Niebuhrian perspectives have influenced his scholarship in the field of history.

Marsden's closing challenge to scholars in economics and other disciplines was to "think hard" about the relationship of their religious faith to their scholarship. The difficulty is that many Christians in the academy "have a Ph.D. in their discipline and a Sunday-school knowledge of their faith." For the "outrageous idea" to bear fruit, Christians must engage the intellectual resources of their Christian faith-traditions more deeply. The remainder of this book is organized around three broad roles of the economist as seen by the editors of this volume: mainstream scholar, policy advocate, and philosopher.

ECONOMIST AS MAINSTREAM SCHOLAR

One of the main priorities for a Christian economist is to be a good economist—both as a teacher and a scholar. It is important that Christian economists serve the profession faithfully, to paraphrase Scripture, as if serving the Lord (Col 3:23). Given the traditional manner whereby ideas are communicated and thought influenced, it is important that Christian economists excel in their discipline as it is understood among mainstream economists. If their voice is to be heard on issues of the integration of faith and learning, they must gain the respect of fellow economists by contributing valuable ideas to the profession via participating in the general discussion.

Given the way that research filters down from scholars at the major research universities to other universities and colleges, it is important that Christians have a presence at the more prestigious research universities. Dedicated scholars surrounded by other dedicated scholars and dedicated students can have a substantial impact. But it is important that the Christian economist at these institutions have an understanding of how Christian convictions affect academic thought, shape a research agenda, and impact the way one interprets the rules of scholarship and, maybe more importantly, empirical results.

If mainstream scholarship is the extent of the impact of Christianity on the profession, many will be disappointed. While an important element of the overall mission, mainstream scholarship done by Christian economists has much the same look and feel as that done by non-Christians. Christian scholarship in economics can encompass so much more. Perhaps Christian colleagues in other disciplines, such as political theory, moral philosophy, Christian ethics, and theology, can help Christian economists have a broader and deeper vision.

Judith M. Dean clearly delineates three roles that dominate the lives of the Christian economist—physician, policy advocate, and philosopher. By physician she means research physician or someone who investigates the origins and development of economic "diseases." She argues that a Christian who is an economist fills a physician's role by studying economic problems, their origins, their evolution, how they can be prevented, and how they respond to various "cures." The resulting scholarship is typically what one recognizes as the mainstream of economics. While the technical standards of mainstream research do not have specifically Christian character, the Christian scholar makes no compromise by adhering to these standards.

At times, Christian economists operate at the level of policy advocate or even philosopher. However, unless these endeavors are backed by first-rate research, results may seem shallow or misdirected. Christian faith may influence one's research topic and research questions. Once these are decided, the goal of the faithful scholar is to conduct research regarded as impeccable within the academy.

How then does Christian faith influence scholarship? Dean proposes three possibilities: If Christians are faithful and allow their beliefs to influence their scholarship, research topics will reflect God's priorities, research questions will be formulated to address those priorities, and proposed solutions will be evaluated in terms of equity as well as efficiency.

The reader should emerge from Dean's paper with a greater appreciation of the challenges facing a Christian scholar and with a better understanding of the importance of conducting quality research as recognized by the economic mainstream. Dean argues that there is no compromise when a Christian economist does technical research that is virtually indistinguishable from that done by a non-Christian. In fact, it is essential that Christians actively produce high-quality, technical research on important issues that affect the world—issues that the Bible stresses, including the environment, debt forgiveness, health care, and poverty. If Christians do not provide society with good research on these issues, then mainstream research will be dominated by perspectives that may ignore or at least minimize the principles that serve to guide Christians' interactions with one another. The profession needs Christians involved in mainstream research. If they are not doing mainstream research, their voices will be silent when important policy decisions are made.

ECONOMIST AS POLICY ADVOCATE

As policy advocate, the Christian economist must evaluate how religious beliefs affect value judgments and in turn the normative issues on which policy prescriptions are based. In spite of the influence of eminent scholars such as Milton Friedman, economists have become more careful in their claims that economics may be practiced in a value-neutral environment (McCloskey, 1983; Wilber & Hoksbergen, 1986).

Recognizing that policy making can never be completely value neutral, Christian economists should contribute to the policy-making process. Policy will be grounded in values. Incorporating Christian values into economic policy will depend on the active participation of Christians in the policy-making process.

Much of the writing on economic policy done by Christians has focused almost exclusively on commentary about social problems, but it has been lacking in scholarly rigor. The importance of numerous Christian scholars from a variety of disciplines contributing to the U.S. debate on controversial economic issues such as discrimination, poverty, welfare, income distribution, immigration, economic development, and health care cannot be overemphasized. The contributions need to be scholarly–historically based, empirical, and targeted for publication in top-quality, peer-reviewed journals.

In her paper, Rebecca Blank contrasts two views of human behavior: what economics teaches and what Christianity teaches. Her presentation is based on the book she coauthored with William McGurn (2004), entitled *Is the Market Moral? A Dialogue on Religion, Economics, and Justice.* Blank emphasizes the importance of thorough understanding of the competitive economic model. The ability to explain and predict the behavior of economic decision-makers is the basis of the model's analytical power. With no central direction, markets use individual self-interest to ensure efficient outcomes.

After summarizing the basic principles of the introductory economics course, Blank challenges some of the basic behavioral assumptions critical to the neoclassical economic paradigm—that more is better and that economic decision-making is dominated by self-interest. In developing her arguments, she addresses how Christian principles define behavior differently. Key elements missing from the economic model are then discussed: first, Christianity calls people into community with one another, a concept that might be better understood by the secular world as "social solidarity." Second, Christianity calls people to be other-interested, not merely self-interested. The second great commandment of Matthew 22:39 makes it clear that Christians are to love their neighbor as themselves. Third, Christians are to measure the abundance of their lives, not in material terms, but in spiritual terms. While the material is not unimportant, it is not the most important. Fourth, the choices Christians make are not morally neutral. The attempt by mainstream economists to separate the positive from the normative is an attempt to deny Christians' call to morality. Finally, the Christian faith demands concern for the poor and disaffected.

Blank then discusses several policy challenges facing the United States today, including full employment, caring for the weak, preservation of the environment, wealth, prosperity, and economic growth. After laying out these policy challenges, she provides insights from the Bible, Christian theologians, and Christian economists. She concludes with a discussion of how one might place into practice an emphasis on the interests of others in a global economy. Globalization has changed the way Christians interact with one another and makes it difficult to maintain a Christian influence in the worldwide economic community.

Can one be a Christian and believe in market solutions to the economic problems of the twenty-first century? To that question Blank adds, Given the sinfulness of human beings, can people be both Christian and human at the same time? She answers both questions in the affirmative. Market outcomes are rarely either good or bad. They are usually good and bad. Christianity requires Christians to be in the world, and yet not to be worldly. They have no choice but to participate in markets, and they must find ways to make markets work for the betterment of all humanity.

Glenn Loury examines the connection between work and faith by addressing the advocacy role of the Christian economist in public policy matters. Loury argues that doing the analytical work of an economist—studying issues such as markets, consumer behavior, and rational choice—is by itself inadequate when it comes to social policy-making. He uses racial profiling as an example of good economic analysis reaching the wrong conclusion. He makes the case that the purview of social science can only capture a portion of the human experience. Questions of incentives and efficiency provide a fundamentally different perspective on the human experience than questions of spiritual identity.

Loury argues that significant, even critical economic issues can and should be addressed from a Christian perspective. If Christians ignore the fact that they are spiritual creatures, they do injustice to the study of economics and to societies that look to economists for useful advice concerning the gamut of social problems.

Loury's paper is based on his book *The Anatomy of Racial Inequality* (2002), and in it, he carefully addresses the political economy of race in America. Aiming to answer three important questions, Loury challenges his reader to think about the human experience in terms of the relational as well as the transactional aspects of the economic experience. The questions he addresses are as follows: What is race? Why is racial inequality so stubbornly persistent? In what does racial justice consist?

Challenging the orthodoxies of the political Left and Right, Loury's approach to these questions is sometimes provocative, often controversial, but always true to his Christian principles. Using an economist's approach, Loury describes the vicious cycle of misinformation that has resulted in racial stereotyping that rationalizes and sustains discrimination. He argues that the Christian desire for fairness and individual freedom and dignity will remain unfulfilled without some forms of race-based intervention. Loury's paper challenges Christian scholars in every discipline to step up and be heard on important social issues that plague modern-day society.

ECONOMIST AS PHILOSOPHER

As philosopher, the Christian economist must evaluate from a Christian perspective the philosophical presuppositions underlying the foundations of economics. The challenge for Christian economists is to offer a new paradigm so closely attuned to reality that it will actually influence the discipline.

The new paradigm may take the form of a critique of the neoclassical approach to understanding economic decision-making. This new approach, heavily steeped in utilitarianism, has fostered an attitude of cynicism among both students and professionals that actually undermines faith in the market system (Frank, Gilovich, & Regan, 1993, 1996). Developing a model of economic behavior that establishes the supremacy of moral principles over narrow self-interest would go a long way in restoring confidence in market principles. How should moral philosophy or Christian ethics properly inform the work of Christian economists?

While self-interest dominates some spheres of economics, cooperative solutions to economic problems cannot be ruled out. Recognizing this, economists should resist an imperialistic attitude that downplays the evidence of cooperative human behavior shown in areas traditionally studied by other disciplines (Lazear, 2000). Economic imperialism not only alienates colleagues in other disciplines, notably political scientists and sociologists, it ignores their contributions toward informing economists about important issues that affect the world community.

While all plenary speakers at the Christianity and Economics Conference touched on matters of philosophy of economics, Michael Novak of the American Enterprise Institute delivered the broadest philosophical reflection. As author of *The Spirit of Democratic Capitalism* (1982) and numerous other books and articles, Novak has reflected and written over many years on the philosophy of economics. Novak's philosophy comes out of his particular experience. Neither he nor the editors claim that what is offered here is a definitive philosophy of economics. Novak is not formally educated in economics. (One might speculate on whether such an education would have been a benefit or detriment to Novak's philosophical development.) Rather, Novak's graduate academic training was in religion and philosophy of religion.

Novak's philosophy is an expression of his intellectual journey from sympathy with pervasive collective control of the economy to an embrace of market capitalism as the most effective way to organize contemporary economies. Novak came to the study of economics from questioning the statist bent of many of his contemporaries—particularly those in religious and clerical circles. He divides his philosophical inquiry into three parts: (1) the adjudication among economic ideologies, (2) the delineation of necessary concepts for consideration of any economic system, and (3) facing particular questions regarding a particular economic system. Most of the essay explores the first and the third parts.

Regarding adjudication among economic ideologies, Novak considers the two major contenders: broad government control of the economic process, and decentralized private markets or capitalism. Novak takes the reader along his intellectual journey from a tenuous embrace of the former to growing conviction about the positive attributes of capitalism. He states that as a young man and a student, "I was strongly pulled toward socialism, but something warned me to hold back" (below, p. 75). So he decided to take on a personal study of economics. Novak acknowledges the strong influence of Peter Berger, Sidney Hook, and F. A. Hayek. Writers with collectivist attachments—Irving Howe, Stuart Hampshire, Michael Harrington, and Robert Heilbroner—were also important to his exploration of economics.

In the end, of course, Novak was drawn to capitalism, with the most extensive statement of his conclusions in *The Spirit of Democratic Capitalism.* Key considerations that buttress Novak's philosophy of economics include opportunity for rising material standards of living for the world's poor, the implications of utopian intellectual attachments, the cultural and political agendas of advocates of socialism, the role of knowledge in the economic process, the connection between economic freedom and political and civic freedom, and the role of mediating institutions in society.

The second level of the philosophy of economics presented by Novak is determining the basic concepts that are relevant to consideration of the economic system. Novak acknowledges that conceptually this level of discourse would come first. However, Novak's own intellectual journey began with judging economic systems—in particular capitalism and socialism. Some relevant concepts for considering all economic systems will be narrowly economic, such as scarcity, trade-offs, and full employment. But there are also many relevant concepts outside the narrow core of economics, such as family, creativity, equality, and liberty. The challenge in this area of the philosophy of economics is to determine the relevant concepts and come to agreement on definitions of these concepts.

The third level of philosophical inquiry involves answering particular questions or challenges regarding an economic system. Novak is concerned about continuing challenges to capitalism, in particular the continued hostility to capitalism in religious quarters. Even with the fall of Soviet communism, the challenge from the religious proceeds unabated.

Novak attempts to answer such criticism in his response to an article by Joerg Rieger (2002) of the Perkins School of Theology at Southern Methodist University. He engages Reiger in debates on the cultural impact of business advertising, historical changes in the level of economic welfare, contemporary inequalities in material well-being, the cultural core of capitalism, and the impact of capitalism on the environment. Throughout, Novak offers a spirited philosophical statement of his journey from socialist sympathy to advocating capitalism and its political and cultural corollaries.

As with his two books on the relationship between economics and religion, Robert Nelson's essay is highly provocative. His first book *Reaching for Heaven on Earth: The Theological Meaning of Economics* (1991) was followed by *Economics as Religion: From Samuelson to Chicago and Beyond* (2002). He states in the latter: "Any economist, whether Christian or non-Christian, who actively participates in the current American economics profession is helping to advance the further marginalization of Christianity" (p. 2) and "The university had become the new seminary for modern secular religion" (p. 10). Like Novak, Nelson recounts his personal intellectual journey. Unlike Novak, Nelson did partake of education in economics, with a Ph.D. from Princeton.

Nelson recounts the story of a conventionally trained economist—in the neoclassical tradition with a heavy dose of econometrics—who finds within his profession the fundamental elements of a religion. This religion of economics is found to be in conflict with the tenets of Christianity. Nelson's story is all the more remarkable since he is not himself a professing Christian.

Nelson begins by sketching his perspective on the relationship between the secular faith of economics and Christianity. He then recounts the culture of his youth, his graduate study at Princeton, and his academic career, which included eighteen years at the U.S. Department of the Interior (which Nelson labels as the Department of Religion). With Nelson's cultural background and training at Princeton, he was well positioned to take his place as a member of the economics wing of the secular academy. However, that was not to be. Nelson's doubts and detours brought him to be a self-proclaimed "economic theologian."

Other economists unwittingly practice the theology of economics without being aware of what they are doing. One is reminded of John Maynard Keynes's statement in *The General Theory* (1965): "Practical men, who believe themselves to be quite exempt from any intellectual influences, are usually the slaves of some defunct economist" (p. 383). Nelson is asserting a variation of Keynes. The Nelson variation would be, "Contemporary economists, who believe themselves to be quite exempt from any religious influences in their work, are the slaves of the implicit religion of their discipline."

What is this religion of economics? Nelson expresses the core of the religion in the title of his first book, *Reaching for Heaven on Earth* (1991). Every religion has its own teleology, a purpose to which human existence is to be directed. This purpose is to create a heaven on earth. This heaven is defined in terms of material abundance. The economics profession developed during the progressive era of American history, and the faith of the progressive era was one of material progress. Economics and the academy in general continue to embrace this progressive teleology. In the academy, there are many priesthoods that seek to contribute to the realization of material abundance. But the high priests come from the economics profession. The economics profession submits to the "gospel of efficiency and growth." Economists have convinced society that they hold the keys to the desired earthly destination.

In addition to teleology, economic religion has an explanation for bad behavior or sin. The Christian explanation based on human nature and the Fall can safely be set aside for a materialistic explanation. Earthly heaven would be realized through economic growth and higher living standards. Of course, those with a lower standard of living would be frustrated. Out of this frustration would come bad behaviors or sin. An inadequate material standard of living is then the fundamental cause of sin. Economics implies that society can expect sin to diminish with rising living standards.

Just as some Christians experience a crisis of faith in their lives, Robert Nelson experienced a crisis of faith in economics. He cites three experiences that caused him to question the religion of economics: Lyndon Johnson's War on Poverty, U.S.–China policy premised on the salutary effects of China's economic growth, and finally, the events of September 11, 2001.

With misgivings about economics, Nelson left the academy to work in the Department of the Interior from 1975 to 1993. There, Nelson interacted extensively with environmentalists. As an economist trained to believe in economic growth and rising material standards of living, Nelson often found himself at odds with environmentalists who held a secular faith that rejected the progressive tenets of economics in favor of an ultimate goal of preservation of the natural environment. Nelson's contact with the secular religion of environmentalists helped bring him to a reflection on economic theology and a consideration of the relationship between economics and Christianity.

Like George Marsden, Nelson believes Christians should assert themselves in the academy. Nelson believes they can incorporate Christian values since "a value-neutral economics can be of no real benefit to society" (below, p. 88). Nelson would also advocate econometric study of the impact of Christian practices—even differing Christian theologies—on societal outcomes. A more robust inclusion of the concept of social capital in research would also be helpful. The goals of efficiency and utility maximization need not be embraced by the Christian economist, who might focus on other goals such as the development of community. Many will find points of disagreement with Nelson. All will find much food for thought on the place of religion and Christianity within contemporary economics.

Practicing economics is not like practicing any other technical method. Arguably, modern economic theory and practice offers its own worldview, or multiple worldviews, that stand in sharp contrast to the Christian worldview (Nelson, 1996). Economics is an integral part of the overall value system that shapes secular society. It is important that Christian economists establish for themselves a respected place at the academic discussion table as mainstream scholar, policy advocate, and philosopher.

WRAPPING IT ALL UP

Probably the most difficult paper to categorize is David P. Gushee's contribution, a broad reflection on ethical issues relating to the contemporary U.S. economy. Gushee draws on his Baptist tradition to argue that economic ethics must be both Jesus-centered and discipleship-centered. Based on the book he coauthored with Glen Stassen *Kingdom Ethics: Following Jesus in Contemporary Context* (2003), Gushee offers an inquiry into the ethics of Jesus as presented in Scriptures. While he gives detailed attention to the Old and New Testaments, he focuses on Jesus' teachings from the Sermon on the Mount (Matt 5:1–7:29) as a rich source for discerning the economic ethics of Jesus.

In his paper, Gushee addresses attitudes toward wealth and consumer goods, responsibilities to the poor, and norms for economic transactions, arguing that Jesus offered principles for behavior that are just as relevant now as they were when He first offered them, and just as authoritative for anyone who professes allegiance to Him. Gushee proposes that Jesus offered two principal teachings in the area of economic life. First, Jesus confronted economic injustice. He called his followers to a different way, not only in their private lives, but also in their public lives. If justice is to prevail in a sinful world, it is essential that Christians restrain the concentration of political and economic power.

Second, Jesus provided guidance on how to free us from sinful patterns related to our attitude and behavior toward material possessions. Jesus offered a new way of life when he addressed the economic dimensions of their lives. Jesus did not reject personal property but instead rejected selfishness, greed, hoarding, and lack of generosity. Living simply and trusting God to meet our needs frees us to practice generosity and seek justice for the poor and hungry.

The Bible provides abundant teachings about money, wealth, poverty, and greed. Gushee examines five key themes, providing application for Christians' private and public lives.

- Possessions are intrinsically insignificant beyond the basic sufficiency provided by a gracious God.
- Misreading the value of possessions stimulates greed.
- Greed encourages a lifestyle of luxury, pride, hoarding, self-indulgence, oppression, and lack of generosity.

- The deceptive allure of wealth can choke discipleship and imperil the soul.
- Jesus identifies with the poor and promises abundance and justice in a coming "great reversal."

We live in the wealthiest and most powerful nation on earth. Because we have been given so much, much is expected of us. Gushee makes it clear that Jesus has called His followers to seek first His kingdom and its justice. Nothing less than our own redemption and that of the world is at stake.

Chapter 1

Faith-Informed Scholarship

George M. Marsden

INTRODUCTION

For the Christian perspective to become a relevant part of economic scholarship, economists must understand the appropriate ways to integrate their faith into their scholarship. The Christian perspective can make a difference—in the way economists view economics, the way they approach their research, and the importance they place on making their research count in the lives of real people.

One of the keys to being an effective scholar is to ask the right questions. In the case of historians, such questions are often suggested by contrasting the present with the past. If modern people were to travel back to, let us say, the sixteenth or seventeenth century, what would seem peculiar? Or, if they wished to gain perspective on their own society, they could imagine which modern social features would seem very strange to someone from that earlier era—possibly Queen Elizabeth I, Pascal, or Newton. By looking at themselves in the perspective of past societies, people notice things that they take for granted about themselves which a visitor from another age would find very peculiar.

The subject I wish to discuss in this essay is one of those peculiarities. Although I have no expertise with the field of economics, I plan to summarize a number of first principles regarding scholarship in general that might presumably be applied to economics. My observations are drawn in part from my book *The Outrageous Idea of Christian Scholarship* (1997), and some passages here closely resemble some in that work and are used with permission. Other passages resemble those in my essay in *The Future of Religious Colleges* (2002) and are used here with permission.

MARGINALIZATION OF RELIGION IN THE CONTEMPORARY ACADEMY

Almost all Americans claim to believe in God. Two-thirds believe in traditional Christian doctrines. (One wonders how deep such belief goes. As someone has said, the most fundamental question for most Americans is "Where's the mall?") Though much of American religious profession may be of low voltage, nonetheless, even if only half of those who profess traditional religious beliefs were seriously committed, that would still be an impressive percentage. Perhaps a third of Americans would be making the immense claim that there is a being great enough to create this unbelievably vast universe, who at the same time cares for each person. This inconceivably great being is concerned for people's health and welfare and states of mind. Think of that. One would expect such a belief in God to have huge intellectual implications. If vast numbers of Americans believe in such an immensely powerful creator God concerned with everyday affairs, then one would think that belief would change everything else those Americans believe.

Yet in our educational system—when it comes to passing ideas from one generation to the next—most Americans, including many who profess serious religious belief, have almost no room at all for God. Not only do Americans seldom mention God in their public classrooms, they act as though he does not exist. In their places of worship they say that their religion is not just for one day a week, but should influence all that they do. Yet, religion is marginalized in most of education about really important things in life—what people should think about other people, society, politics, economics, careers, the environment, themselves, their moral values, their nature and destiny (if any). Americans teach their young people to think about themselves and their world as though God did not exist.

In his widely read book *The Culture of Disbelief* (1993), Yale law professor Stephen Carter has some helpful observations regarding the current situation. Carter observes that the problem is not so much discrimination against religion in American public life, but its trivialization. Americans express their religious sentiments in public about as freely as in any modern society. ("I just want to thank the Lord that my curveball was breaking real good tonight.") But the religious rhetoric seldom amounts to anything substantial. Religious belief, says Carter, is most often treated as though it were a harmless hobby, like building model airplanes or sailboarding.

This is the way religion is usually handled in most of the U.S. educational system, including higher education. Typically it is treated as an appropriate private hobby—perhaps like the chess club. Administrators at most universities and colleges will encourage voluntary religious organizations on campus. Nevertheless, few people in mainstream higher education would think it appropriate to relate religious belief to academic work. When it comes to learning about the important aspects of life that higher education deals with, belief in God is treated as though it is irrelevant. That is the case, I believe, even at many church-related colleges. Furthermore, many professors who are firm believers in a traditional religious faith would never dream of trying to relate that faith to something as important as their scholarship.

This trivialization of religion in education has a deeper implication. The deeper implication is that in large areas of life Americans are taught that the way to think most deeply about things—despite their religious professions—is to think about them as though God did not exist. That is, at least, the message that most Americans are willing to send to the next generation in our educational system.

A visitor from another era would think that, given Americans' degree of religious profession, their acceptance of an educational system in which belief in God is irrelevant to learning is very strange. Suppose that a scholar such as Socrates, Erasmus, or Descartes were to show up and ask for a tour of campus, and after which his guide explains that, although many Americans believe in God, they do not try to relate that belief to their scholarship. Such a visitor would find that very puzzling.

Reasons for Marginalization of Religion in American Education

There are, of course, some good reasons why American culture arranges things this way. If one looks at the historical developments, these reasons become particularly evident. The displacement of traditional Christianity from the privileged position it held in nineteenth-century academia is readily understandable. Christianity had long been part of a cultural establishment that controlled higher education. Until the rise of universities after the Civil War, most American colleges were under some sort of religious control. Even most state colleges had Protestant clergy as their presidents. Traditional Christianity was often used to restrict academic inquiry. At more conservatively religious schools, traditional Christianity was often part of a defensive posture and was sometimes taught in heavy-handed ways. Academic reformers fought against these restrictive religious establishments and eventually dismantled those that had the largest cultural influence. This reaction was part of the larger process of the disestablishment of Protestantism as semiofficial religion in America.

One can understand this disestablishment in ideological terms as a matter of equity, but one can also see that it had an important economic base and function. The transformation of pre-Civil War Christian colleges into fledgling modern universities after the Civil War was part of the modern nation-building that grew out of the Civil War. The American Civil War took place in the same era as that of national consolidation in Europe, as in Germany and Italy, and reflected something of the same modernizing impulse. The universities were to be designed to serve a modern industrialized economy. Built largely by the Yankee victors in the war, they reflected roughly the same combination of forces that had brought victory to the North: technological superiority plus the moral ideal of freedom.

"Freedom" became the watchword of the new universities and meant two different things. At the ideological level it meant freedom as an ideal for the citizens of the emerging republic. The idea of the free citizen was, of course, connected with ideals of free enterprise, and the leadership of the new universities was overwhelmingly Republican. More important for my purposes, freedom in this era meant objective scientific inquiry. Those who built the modern universities contrasted their emphasis on free inquiry to religious dogmatism—either to Catholic authoritarianism or to earlier Protestant dogmatism. Prior to this era it had been assumed that religion would be a unifying force in a culture, so it was natural to encourage religion in public culture, including higher education. Now, in the process of national consolidation in a pluralistic emerging industrial nation, religion was seen as divisive for the public culture. So the process began of moving substantive religious belief to the private sphere, while mainstream higher education continued as part of the public domain. It is easy to see the economic advantages to encouraging the privatization of religious belief in a pluralistic society. People might be encouraged to have private religious beliefs, but things would run more smoothly if they would learn to keep quiet about religion in the public domain.

There is much to be said for this public–private divide with respect to religion. During a long era of national consolidation and assimilation of diverse groups, it has been an important way of keeping the peace. There are good reasons to have institutions of higher learning that serve the whole public, as well as others that may be defined more by a religious heritage. For those defined as part of the public domain there are, furthermore, legitimate desires to uphold on equity that would put restraints on certain types of religious discourse. For instance, it would be inappropriate at a state university for a teacher to use the classroom to explicitly evangelize according to her religious faith, or to lead students in a prayer asking that they might come to believe that faith.

Defending the Return of Religious Perspectives to the Academy

At the same time that one recognizes the legitimacy of these and similar concerns regarding higher education in the public domain, I want to ask whether our society may not have overcorrected in attempting to eliminate religious perspectives entirely as legitimate academic points of view. Might there not be a place for perspectives that are frankly shaped by religious outlooks, just as there is a place for perspectives that are shaped by other ideologies, outlooks, or social locations? For instance, if there is room for feminist, Marxist, neoconservative, African American, gay, or liberal Democratic perspectives in the academy, why should there not be room as well for various sorts of Jewish, Islamic, Christian, or Buddhist perspectives—so long as the advocates of those perspectives play within the legitimate rules of public academic discourse? Or is there something peculiar about *religious* perspectives that justify their being suppressed in the academy as much as possible, while other diverse perspectives might be welcomed or encouraged?

It might be objected, for instance, that much of faith-informed scholarship depends on claims of revelation, or sources of knowledge not shared by others. Hence it would violate rules essential for promoting fruitful public discourse. The problem is analogous to the problem of introducing special revelations into a court of law. It simply does not advance the discussion to argue on the basis of an authority that some people regard as supreme and others regard as bogus. This seems to be a valid concern so far as it goes. In a pluralistic public setting, it makes sense to have a rule that representatives of various religious beliefs not argue primarily on the basis of the authority of their special or private revelations.

That being granted, another category of scholarship that relates revelatory claims to research scholarship shaped by background religious commitments should not be objectionable. One's worldview may be fundamentally shaped by beliefs that ultimately rest on claims to revelation or other sources of authority not shared by most people. For instance, a Mennonite might believe that all warfare is wrong because it violates a command of Jesus. Or a Dorothy Day might think that Jesus' commands dictate that one should take a stand for racial justice or care for the poor. Other Christians might hold that God's revelation shows that humans are naturally corrupt and that one should be suspicious of utopian hopes that presume a general improvement in human behavior. Still others may believe, on the contrary, that revelation shows that there is hope for a general improvement in human behavior.

Any of these viewpoints might be introduced for religious reasons into the mainstream academy, but defended with arguments and evidence that are publicly accessible. So having a religious *source* for one's views does not automatically exclude one's views from acceptance in the academy so long as one argues for them on other, more widely accessible, grounds.

Despite the fact that people might not articulate some of their background beliefs as evidence or arguments in pluralistic academic settings, these beliefs still may play a significant role. Nicholas Wolterstorff (1984) refers to these significant background beliefs as "control beliefs."[1] Such beliefs, even if not directly expressed, act as significant controls on what other beliefs and theories people are willing to entertain. Or the presence of these background control beliefs in one's web of beliefs may affect the relative importance assigned to other beliefs.

[1]Wolterstorff himself makes a distinction between "control beliefs" and "background beliefs," placing less controversial beliefs (such as that I am essentially the same person today as I was yesterday) in the latter category. Control beliefs, in his terminology, also do not have to remain in the background. What I am talking about here might be more precisely called "background control beliefs."

It is, of course, fair game in academia to uncover and to attack the background control beliefs that account for a fellow academic's dogmatism. If one can show that a colleague's controversial opinions are grounded on a blind allegiance to racism, Marxism, liberalism, humanism, anything French and obscure, or to a religious dogma, one may have a reason to be suspicious of such views.

Nonetheless, in cases of allegiance to ideologies such as those just mentioned, the love of one's basic commitments is not necessarily blind. On the one hand, each of these views rests on foundations that are ultimately mysterious, rather than scientific: so do liberal pragmatic or postmodern deconstructionist views. On the other hand, there are versions of each of these viewpoints, carefully reasoned and weighed against other sources of knowledge, which can be shown to rest on no shakier ground than that of some of the most widely accepted views in the academy. If representatives of such views, including religiously based views, are willing to play by the other rules of the academy, there seems no reason why they should be discredited just because their views involve some background dogmatism.

At this point it is sometimes objected that religious beliefs simply in the background of academics' thought are not particularly relevant to actual scholarship. This objection may especially be heard in a field like economics where a large part of the discipline involves technical expertise and in that sense might be regarded as scientific or objective. This same objection is common in the study of history. Secular colleagues claim they do not see that Christianity makes much difference in the scholarship of authors who profess to be Christians, because Christians seem to present their history using the same standards as everyone else.

In my opinion the reason the impact of faith-informed perspectives is not always immediately evident is that religious perspectives are not the *only* perspectives that inform a religious person's scholarship. As an historian who is religious, my standards for evaluating historical events are shaped by *multiple* traditions of which my religious perspective is just one. To keep it simple, I am shaped by, among other things, aspects of American political liberalism, aspects of the culture of modern science, Reformed Christianity, and traditions of the *craft* of modern professional history in which I have been trained. I want to underscore the role of the tradition of a craft. Like historians of other persuasions who have learned their craft in the academic mainstream, I look at natural causes of human behavior, and I work according to widely accepted rules of argument and evidence that can be understood and evaluated by people from many evaluative traditions. In a field like economics, the expectations of what one does will meet even more precise technical and scientific standards.

Nonetheless, even granting that most of what one does will be such technical analysis, religious faith commitments are likely to influence in at least four pervasive ways the evaluative dimensions of doing the craft. These sorts of influences are no better illustrated than in the topics of most of the papers presented in the conference on which this book is based.

1. What do I think important enough to study?
2. What questions do I ask about it?
3. What currently fashionable interpretive strategies are compatible with my religious outlook?
4. How do I, implicitly or explicitly, evaluate scholarly developments as positive in terms of my religious outlook?

I also need to mention three provisos that are essential to understanding the extent of the influence of religiously based evaluative standards:

1. Religious perspective will change some things, but not everything. For example, in history it does not change the way I calculate the date that Washington crossed the Delaware. Yet my normative commitments will shape the amount of emphasis I put on that event and the nuances of evaluating it. Do we put emphasis on Washington or on the common soldier doing the crossing? Was it a heroic act of patriotism or a terrorist act to attack Hessians when they were celebrating Christmas?
2. For religiously based evaluations to be operative, there is no requirement that the evaluations be unique. Think again of a pacifist Mennonite historian and suppose that she is evaluating America's participation in World War II. The fact that a secular antiwar activist agreed with her would not make the Mennonite's reasons for condemning the war any less Mennonite.
3. It is also very important to bear in mind that there is no single faith-informed perspective. Rather, there is as much variety among faith-informed perspectives as there is among secular perspectives. Even considering Christianity alone, there are countless perspectives that might inform one's scholarship. Often the debates *within* a tradition are the most stimulating and creative.

VARIETIES OF RELIGIOUSLY INFORMED SCHOLARSHIP

This last point brings me to the question of the agendas that ought to grow out of these basic principles. First, Christian academics should not think so much in terms of "Christianity" and their discipline, but in terms of a *particular Christian intellectual tradition* and their discipline. One reason for this is simply modesty. If each Christian academic spoke of his perspective on the welfare state as "the Christian view," he would be presumptuous, since there are multiple Christian views. More importantly, it is helpful to think explicitly about the *specific* Christian traditions that are shaping academic thought.

I can best illustrate by reflecting on the traditions that shape my own scholarship. As I stated earlier, my outlook is not shaped only by my Christianity, but also by a number of other commitments that grow out of my social location and my involvement in the historian's craft. Nonetheless my viewpoint is influenced by more than a generic "Christianity." Rather, it is shaped by a number of specific Christian subtraditions, including the Augustinian, the Kuyperian, and a bit of the influence of Reinhold Niebuhr (or at least my imperfect and selective understandings of these traditions).

The first two of these subtraditions emphasize both creation and regeneration. So my epistemology tends toward a chastened realism. Because people are beings created by a benevolent Creator, I think they can communicate with people from other traditions and engage in things like historical study with some degree of objectivity. Contrary to the postmodernists, I do not believe that people can create their own realities. God is the creator of a common reality. Yet, as I have been arguing, whatever degree of objectivity inherent in human perspectives, including faith perspectives, people often substantially limit themselves from experiencing that reality. This can occur when people's perspectives control what they are looking for and hence what they see.

I can best address this point from my own work, *The Soul of the American University* (1994), which chronicles the history of religion in education. One of the main questions I ask throughout that book is why early American educators did not do more to integrate their faith and learning. People outside the Kuyperian tradition seldom ask this question. Because of my tradition, my whole exploration of American higher education in the seventeenth through mid-nineteenth century is built around this question—why during this era of Protestant establishment was integration of faith and learning usually so inadequate? As I stated at the beginning of this essay, one of the basic questions that has shaped my historical inquiries into American higher education has been my curiosity about how easily most Americans accept the separation of their religious faith from their higher learning. Noticing that phenomenon as a problem, rather than as a natural occurence, grows directly out of my Kuyperian Reformed tradition.

Another theological perspective that deeply influences the structure of *The Soul of the American University* is a modern-day version of the Augustinian principle of the two cities. In my appropriation of this theme, Christians are at their best when they live in constructive tension with the dominant culture. They are often at their worst when they themselves are an establishment. In my view, Roger Williams is more a hero than is John Winthrop. I tried to make sure that nobody would miss this point by adding the book's subtitle, *From Protestant Establishment to Established Nonbelief.*

My tradition of Kuyperian Christianity also involves commitments to a just and pluralistic society. So I repeatedly emphasize the irony of a Protestant establishment that built a Christian society through excluding Jews, Catholics, and others. Recognition of the discriminatory dimension built into mainstream Protestant higher education was one of the major factors forcing Protestantism's disestablishment. I present this disestablishment as a good development with ironic consequences. Particularly, laudable zeal to ensure than no *one* religion be established eventually led to an overcorrection that left the academy with inadequate ways to accommodate varieties of faith-informed scholarship.

Another Christian perspective that shapes my evaluations is a combination of a Niebuhrian and Calvinist view of human nature. I see humans as deeply flawed, often in ironic ways, and Christians as by no means immune from this defect. In agreement with Reinhold Niebuhr, I believe that the greatest injustices are often done in the name of good causes. So my interpretation of the history and demise of the Protestant educational establishment is built around that ironic theme. In the stories I tell, well-intentioned decisions often have unintended or unperceived consequences. Also, especially when tied to power as it was historically in higher education, Christianity tends to be used as a means to further self-interests.

It should be evident from these several examples that, although I practice the craft of history in ordinary ways, my narratives are shaped significantly by some very particular theological commitments. They are of course shaped by other commitments as well, but certainly the theological ones have pervasive influences in each of the four ways mentioned above. In my past research, they determined the subject that I chose. They shaped the questions I asked about the subject. They guided my choices of interpretive strategies. They determined how I evaluated my subjects.

Admittedly some disciplines and some topics within those disciplines allow more room for significant Christian perspectives than do others. Just as feminist influence is most likely to emerge in topics where gender is an explicit issue, so religious perspectives emerge most clearly when religion is explicitly in view. But various religious perspectives will also shape a wide range of scholarship involving moral judgments—or even simply a set of priorities about what should be studied. It is also easy, of course, to think of areas in any discipline where traditionally religious perspectives do not dramatically change the way one does the craft. Yet the number of places where traditionally religious perspectives can foster new critical outlooks is adequate for the enterprise to have great potential.

THE CHALLENGE OF RELIGIOUSLY INFORMED SCHOLARSHIP

I have argued first that such faith-informed perspectives are legitimate within the mainstream academy, and second that they can make a substantial difference in some important aspects of most disciplines. If my reader is willing to grant those conclusions, then the next question is where to go from here. One answer, of course, is to hold conferences such as the one that led to this book. More broadly, the practical implication is that scholars, including teachers and students, should be encouraged to think hard about the relationship of their religious faith to their disciplines, rather than be discouraged from considering the connection, as is now generally the case in public culture. Inevitably religious faith will influence scholarship in some ways anyway, since faith forms an important part of the identities of many people. But often that relationship is haphazard and superficial. Often, because scholars have not thought hard about the relationship, the intellectual strength of the faith side is vastly inadequate. Many academics have difficulty appreciating the potentialities for relating their learning to their faith because they have a Ph.D. in their discipline and a Sunday-school knowledge about their faith. In order to correct that balance they need substantial study of the intellectual resources that their faith has to offer.

It is for that reason I say that the main thing that needs to be done is for scholars in fields like economics to educate themselves in the intellectual dimensions of their religious heritage. If their heritage lacks such dimensions, then they should adopt aspects of others that do have sophisticated traditions of thinking about such issues, such as Catholic, Anabaptist, or Reformed. Christians simply need to do their homework on the faith side of the equation relating Christian faith to scholarship.

As I see it, Christians must assert the legitimacy of faith as part of the academic enterprise in a public academic culture that is not used to thinking hard about such issues. Forty years ago gender was an important factor shaping scholarship, but not many people openly acknowledged the implications of gender for their scholarship. Today, people almost universally recognize that such inquiry has enriched academia, even if sometimes at the expense of excessive claims. I see no good reason why faith-informed perspectives should not be at least equally enriching, even if Christians too have to guard against excesses. Many religious traditions have substantial intellectual heritages that can be related with rigor to current academic issues. Furthermore, it simply makes good sense that, if religious faith is an important part of the identity and social location of many people, those people should be encouraged to think about how their faith relates to higher learning. If, as I said at the beginning, one believes in a God who has created this unimaginably vast universe and yet cares about individual humans, then that belief should make an important difference in how one thinks about the most significant questions studied at the highest levels of education. If one believes in such a God, then it should make some difference as to what else one thinks. The challenge as Christian scholars is to put in the hard work it takes to figure out what that difference should be.

With these first principles in mind, this book now addresses the challenges of implementing them into the practice of economic scholarship. If the Christian perspective has a legitimate place at the discussion table, how best do Christians take advantage of their rightful place and convince the academic community that they deserve to be heard? The next five chapters address the various roles that economic scholars fill and how best to enter the intellectual discourse and ensure that the Christian perspective can make a difference in the work Christians perform.

Chapter 2

The Christian Economist as a Mainstream Scholar

Judith M. Dean

INTRODUCTION

To have influence in the academic discussion, it is important to excel in one's discipline. It takes quality scholarship, as defined by the mainstream, to get a seat at the discussion table. Without the respect earned in the mainstream it is nearly impossible to get an audience when one attempts to interject a Christian worldview into the discussion.[1]

The purpose of this essay is to discuss the role of the Christian economist as a mainstream scholar. To highlight the importance of this issue, let me begin with a few difficult questions. "If I were to take your course in econometrics, would I be able to tell you are a Christian?" This question was put to me a few years ago by a new graduate of Gordon College (my alma mater)—a college known for its emphasis on integration of faith and learning. Assuming that the student meant the content of the econometrics course, I replied, "Probably not.

[1]This essay is an extension of "Being a Good Physician: Reflections on Christianity and Economic Research," prepared for "Christian Economists Doing Economics: A View from the Trenches," a conference sponsored by the Dept. of Economics, Wheaton College, and the Association of Christian Economists, January 1998, Chicago, Ill. Much of my thinking on this subject took shape at SAIS, Johns Hopkins University, where I was Associate Professor of Economics from 1990–2000. The views expressed in this essay are solely those of the author. They do not represent the views of the International Trade Commission, or the views of any of the individual commissioners.

But, if you were to watch C. Everett Koop doing surgery on a child, could you tell he was a Christian?" This conversation made me think. What should my classroom be like if I am a Christian and an economist? If my answer to the student is correct, does this mean that I am keeping my secular profession insulated from my Christian profession when I teach?

A colleague at Johns Hopkins University put another difficult question to me: "Are your views on international trade and economic development similar to Jagdish Bhagwati?" Bhagwati is an internationally famous professor of international trade and economic development; I have great respect for him, and I find myself in agreement with a large part of his published work. But Bhagwati does not profess to be a Christian. In fact, he has referred to his Hindu background in some of his work. Does the fact that Bhagwati and I have very similar views mean that my approach to my field—and therefore my own research work—is in some sense completely secular?

These questions highlight a serious dilemma. Should the content of Christians' technical courses and technical research look different if they are believers? If the content does not look different—if it looks "mainstream"—have Christians compromised their faith? My answer is no. There is no compromise when a Christian economist engages in mainstream research or teaching.[2] This is the first proposition, which I hope to be able to demonstrate in the following pages.

More recently, two other difficult questions provoked me to think more about this subject. The first question came from a Christian professor organizing a symposium for an institute at Gordon College. She asked if I knew of any Christian economists doing research on global warming who could debate a prominent scientist in that field. Because I had worked on trade and environmental issues for quite awhile, I knew of many people who studied the economics of global warming. However, to my knowledge none of them were believers. After much searching, the conference organizer chose an internationally known non-Christian economist in that field. Why could I not supply the conference organizer with names? Why are believers not contributing to the research in this area?

The second question came from a faculty member at Wheaton College. He invited me to participate in a symposium on debt forgiveness, along with some representatives from Jubilee 2000 (Center for Applied Christian Ethics, 2000). Jubilee is an umbrella group for many Christian organizations and private citizens advocating debt forgiveness. The question was, Should the United States forgive developing country debt? The symposium took place in October of 2000, as two bills on debt forgiveness sat in Congress (U.S. Congress, 1999; U.S. Senate, 1999). Congress itself was debating what nature of debt forgiveness the United States should adopt. Jubilee made a big impact on the U.S. Congress. They also made a big impact on the World Bank by their pressure and

[2]Since I was asked to focus on research, this essay will not pursue the topic of teaching in any depth. However, the propositions made here could also be applied to questions regarding teaching and course content.

their publicity. But most of the supporters of Jubilee and most of those involved do not have any formal training in economics in general, let alone training on the issue of debt. Again, I began to wonder: Where are the Christian economists? Why are they not involved?

Stewardship of the earth, debt, poverty, and forgiveness are all topics that the Bible asks Christians to take seriously. And yet, it is hard to find Christian economists who are supplying the world with good, technically well-done research on these issues. There is no compromise: Christian economists must be engaged in mainstream research. This is my second proposition.

THERE IS NO COMPROMISE WHEN CHRISTIAN ECONOMISTS ENGAGE IN MAINSTREAM RESEARCH

Wearing Three Hats

Broadly speaking, Christian economists have three roles. I call these the philosopher, the physician, and the advocate. By philosopher, I mean that economists have a responsibility to investigate the extent to which the philosophical presuppositions underlying the foundations of economics are consistent with a Christian worldview. Michael Novak and Rebecca Blank provide a very good understanding of what this means at a macro and micro level, respectively, in their contributions to this book. Christian economists need to approach their field with questions, challenging its philosophical presuppositions. By physician, I have in mind a research physician. I see economists as having responsibility to investigate how economic "diseases" behave, whether or not certain economic policies are appropriate cures, and how certain economic health problems arise and can be prevented. Finally, by policy advocate I mean someone who advocates changes in policies that have detrimental effects, or advocates new policies that address failures in the economic system.

I believe each Christian economist must take on each of these three roles. All have three hats they must wear. However, as a good trade economist, I believe in comparative advantage. And that means that not all Christian economists will do all three things equally well. Some are very well suited to doing the more philosophically challenging research. While some will dabble in that, others will publish books on the subject. Some are much better at doing the technical research in the physician type of role, and perhaps will not spend as much of their research time on policy advocacy or philosophical work. The same holds true for the role of policy advocate. In other words, I do not believe in complete specialization. Christian economists need to be actively pursuing work related to all three roles, though they will clearly spend more time on one and less on the others, based on the abilities God has given them. Whether they wear the philosopher, physician, or advocate hat, it is imperative that their faith have an influence on their work. The form that influence takes will differ depending on which hat they are wearing. The challenge they face is to integrate their faith with their work, no matter which of these roles they happen to be playing.

Now here is the problem as I see it. Christian economists have spent most of their time being philosophers. Many people, some of whom will likely read this essay, have done very good work showing how philosophical analysis brings to light certain problems for the Christian economist. The trouble is—as George Marsden points out in his essay—Christian economists often lack the philosophical training to do it well. They attempt this kind of work with an introductory level of philosophical training, along with a doctorate in economics. In contrast, they have generally left the work of the research physician to the secular world. Yet most doctoral programs have well equipped the Christian economist to do the research-physician-type work—mainstream research. Finally, Christian economists have left policy advocacy, generally speaking, to the theologians and the sociologists.[3] Yet they often lack the economic training to address well economic policy issues.

Seeing Mainstream Research Through a Different Lens

I would like to urge Christian economists to look at mainstream research through a different lens. I suggest that a more productive way for Christians to interact with mainstream economic research is to think of themselves as research physicians, with the patients being economies. A physician's role is to improve the health of the community that he or she serves. To do this, some physicians must devote themselves to research on diseases, others study medications, and some focus on prevention. Now this does not mean that that each physician would not see patients and care about individuals. But some of them must be doing the research, or else the doctors sitting in clinics would have nothing to do. They would not have the right tools. This kind of research physician work requires a sound understanding of the human body—how it functions when it is healthy, and how it functions when it is not. It also requires the ability to carry out empirical work to test the validity of hypotheses and the effectiveness of medications.

This is not that different from what Christian economists working on mainstream research are trying to do. They are trying to improve the health of the economy. The Scriptures make clear that certain economic issues are priorities—the welfare of the poor, the carrying out of economic justice, and the stewardship of the physical world, just to name a few. The neglect of these priorities in U.S. and other societies should be seen rather like a disease that needs to be addressed. Economists should approach them the way a research physician might respond to an outbreak of malaria in a small village in Africa, saying, I've got to do something. It seems to me that if Christians think about mainstream research in this way, they will understand that they need to actively pursue it to wisely carry out their responsibilities as Christians.

[3]Two good examples of this would be Tony Campolo and Ron Sider. They have both been outspoken on issues of poverty, wealth, and the church, yet neither of them are economists.

What will this require? First, it will require that Christians use training in theoretical economics to work out a thorough understanding of the problem at hand and the implications of any proposed solutions. Glenn Loury's essay on racial inequality in this book is an excellent example. He is using his training in labor economics to think through the problem of racial discrimination, and to assess the implications of affirmative action and other policy proposals. Another excellent example is Pedro Pallares's discussion of poverty in Mexico (2003). He argues that macroeconomic solutions to poverty will not solve Mexico's poverty problem. The solution lies in getting down to a very micro level and understanding poverty's fundamental causes. Interestingly, this is something that other economists have also concluded, after much research. Even multilateral agencies like the World Bank have determined that though macrostabilization may be necessary, it is not sufficient to resolve the poverty issue in most of the world. Instead one needs to turn to more fundamental causes, like the lack of physical and human capital on the part of individuals, and try to address them. This is just the kind of application of theoretical training that Christian economists should undertake.

Secondly, Christian economists will need to use their empirical skills to assess the effects of different policy proposals and to work out their implications for different groups in society. There are many good examples to illustrate this point, but one that immediately comes to my mind is the issue of child labor. There has been fascinating recent work on the effects of prohibiting child labor in places like Pakistan. Due to pressure from the West, some places have actually imposed such prohibitions. Interestingly enough, empirical work on small villages in Pakistan has shown that prohibitions have produced lower levels of income for children and their families. This has sometimes caused more children to enter the workforce, or existing child laborers to take on multiple jobs. In other words, the empirical evidence shows the problem is exacerbated, not ameliorated, by prohibitions. This is exactly the kind of thing Christian economists need to do with empirical training and tools. They should be asking whether certain policies really work—whether they are the right cure for the disease. For that they need to use their training in what they normally think of as mainstream research. If Christians take good theoretical and empirical training and actually apply it in this way, they will be better equipped to offer wise counsel to policymakers. In other words, they will have something to offer in that third role as an advocate.

Thinking Faithfully about Mainstream Research

I mentioned earlier that no matter which hat Christians are wearing, their faith should permeate their work. This is absolutely essential. How does Christian faith impact mainstream research? I'm going to echo to some degree what George Marsden has written already, but I think he is absolutely right. The impact of one's Christianity in mainstream research work is not necessarily evidenced by a difference in technical methodology from secular counterparts. Just as the Christian research physician working on a cure for malaria has the same kind of laboratory equipment that a Hindu might, a Christian economist and a Hindu economist will likely use the same statistical tools or economic models to test the implications of a particular policy.

How, then, do Christians see their faith affecting their mainstream work? First of all, as George Marsden argued during the conference, it manifests itself in the choice of research topics. I interpret that statement to mean that Christians' choices will reflect God's priorities. One can think of many examples from the Scriptures that indicate areas of economic work important to God, and therefore important to Christian economists.

Secondly, faith will influence the formulation of research questions. C. Stephen Evans (1999), a philosopher at Baylor, makes the point that Christians' choice of definitions of terms should be affected by their faith. I think he is correct. When I formulate my research question, the terms I choose and the way I define them should be influenced by my faith. C. S. Lewis had a brilliant way of taking an issue and then helping the reader ask the right questions to reach a thorough understanding of the problem.

Thirdly, Christians' faith is seen in the way they evaluate potential solutions to problems. Paraphrasing James Sauer (2002), evaluation of potential solutions should use both transcendent and immanent criteria. In other words, Christians need to bring into play both criteria from economics, such as efficiency, and ideas of transcendent criteria, such as ethical treatment of human beings when evaluating policy prescriptions. Using both these sets of criteria will likely lead to different policy conclusions than if either set of criteria were used alone. It is in at least these three areas—choice of topics, formulation of questions, and evaluation of potential solutions—that Christian faith should impact mainstream research work.

THERE IS NO COMPROMISE: CHRISTIAN ECONOMISTS MUST BE ENGAGED IN MAINSTREAM RESEARCH

The challenge is clear: Christian economists must be engaged in mainstream research. I want to be able to give Gordon College names of Christian economists working on global warming. I want to be able to tell Wheaton that there are Christian economists working on debt forgiveness. So this is more than a challenge. It is perhaps a plea. The following examples will demonstrate the need for Christians to be actively contributing to mainstream economics.

Uruguay Round Agreement on Textiles and Clothing: January 2005

January 2005 signifies the completion of the Uruguay Round Agreement on Textiles and Clothing (ATC). The ATC calls for the removal of nontariff barriers on the imports of textiles and clothing coming into the United States,

Canada, and the European Union. This is actually a very important issue for developing countries. The scope of these restraints is tremendous. The United States alone has agreements restricting trade with approximately 44 countries, covering about 145 products. The effect of these restrictions falls heavily on the many low-skilled workers employed in such industries in developing countries. These trade distortions have been in place for a long time—some developing countries have faced barriers to their textile and apparel exports for almost 30 years.

Until recently almost no research examined the implications of nontariff restrictions for exporting countries. There is now a tremendous amount of research in this area. However, most of it looks at implications for the United States, Canada, and the European Union. Some policymakers have recently argued that most developing countries would end up net losers when the barriers were lifted in January 2005. They believe that without these barriers, China will outcompete all other exporting countries and capture the global market for textiles and apparel. Other policymakers believe that the barriers are no longer significant—they are not really an impediment to trade. The actual outcome after January 2005 will have enormous implications for the poor, and for economic justice as well.

Uruguay Round Agreement on Textiles and Clothing: The Opportunity

Soon after I began working for the U.S. International Trade Commission (USITC), I had several opportunities to contribute to policymakers' understanding of the implications of lifting the trade restrictions on textiles and clothing. As part of the latest USITC biannual report (2002), I estimated the tax equivalents of U.S. textile and apparel trade barriers for all exporting countries and all products. During this project, the U.S. Trade Representative asked the USITC to review the existing literature on the implications of removing these barriers for the exporting countries. The task fell to me.

The Need for Mainstream Research

Without the mainstream research I had already done on this subject, I would have been completely ill equipped to respond to these opportunities. In the 1990s I had done two statistical studies on the impact of such barriers on developing countries, both on their welfare and on the patterns of trade (1990; "Market Disruption," 1995). These were exactly the two topics that I was being asked to explore by the U.S. Trade Representative's office. I also spent some time doing theoretical studies on how this type of barrier (known as a voluntary export restraint) actually affects different exporting countries (Dean & Gangopadhyay, 1991, 1992). It is a very complex system, and its implications for exporters are not obvious. In addition, I had spent significant time reading other scholars' work, regarding the size of these barriers, their significance, and their implications for different types of exporting countries. Without this background, I would not have been able to take up the opportunities before me.

There is no doubt that my faith shaped my mainstream research work. With respect to the USITC study (2002), my faith affected choice of definitions and methodology. There are actually several ad hoc ways in which researchers define which of these barriers impede trade. These methods tend to underestimate the number of barriers that really matter. I chose to use multiple criteria, so that an upper bound and lower bound estimate would be available. I also chose a methodology that would yield as accurate an estimate of these tax equivalents as possible. There was great pressure to do something completely ad hoc and be done with it. But morally, I could not do that. I had to do something that would give the policy community as accurate a picture as possible of the gravity of these trade restraints.

My faith affected the questions I chose to answer, and the results I chose to present. I had to choose the right questions to ask and the appropriate evidence to review, so that an unbiased view would be conveyed. I chose to present a range of results, drawing on the work of many other scholars. I could thus clearly convey where scholars agreed and where they disagreed, how different assumptions might affect scholars' results, and whether the balance of evidence suggested that removal of the barriers could be detrimental to developing countries.

The Issue: Doha Round

The recently completed Doha Ministerial Declaration (2001), describes the agenda for the upcoming round of world trade talks. One of the main issues in the Doha Round, not surprisingly, will be trade and the environment. In Seattle 1999, people in the streets protested—sometimes violently—the launch of a new round of trade talks. Some protesters believed that trade liberalization would be harmful to the environment. Some feared industrial countries would lose from trading with poor countries, because standards on air, water, and other types of pollution are relatively lenient in poor counties compared to the industrialized world. It is possible that free trade agreements and other types of trade reforms could be aborted if such fears ultimately shape policy. Trade barriers previously removed might be reinstated. Harmonization of standards across countries might be forced through the World Trade Organization (WTO). Trade barriers might be allowed as punitive measures against any country perceived to have more lenient standards than the United States or other powerful members of the WTO.

This is another example of the absolutely critical need for good research. These issues impinge on stewardship of the environment and welfare of the poor. Good economic research on the subject, thus far, has shown that a number of the fears voiced by protesters and others are largely unwarranted. For example, rather than improving environmental quality, trade barriers can worsen environmental degradation as well as reduce the welfare of all countries. Harmonization can force inappropriate and expensive standards on poor countries, and can actually inhibit the development of appropriate environmental policy in those countries. Thus, Christian economists have very good reasons to get involved in this work and try to find the right answers to these questions.

The Opportunity

I had a number of opportunities to do just that. I was invited to provide background research on trade and environment for the World Bank's major publication, *The World Development Report 1992.* This led to subsequent requests from the Organization of Economic Cooperation and Development (OECD) and the then Office of Technology Assessment of the U.S. Congress. The World Bank held two conferences on issues of environment and development, in which I was able to participate (Fredriksson, 1999; Low, 1992). More recently I was invited to edit a collection of seminal contributions on trade and the environment for an international environmental reference series (2001). At the USITC a new study of the Free Trade Agreement of the Americas will include an examination of the environmental implications of that agreement. This will likely be required of future free trade agreements, granting further opportunities to look at this issue.

The Need for Mainstream Research

Without my training in mainstream research, I would never have had the initial request from the World Bank, nor been able to carry out an investigation of this subject. I began writing survey papers and theoretical and empirical studies on whether trade liberalization harms the environment ("Export Bans," 1995; 1999a, 2002; Dean & Gangopadhyay, 1997). Very few people had tried to actually test hypotheses on this subject using data from poor countries. So my training in empirical work and willingness to attempt such studies meant an opportunity to discover new evidence and inform the debate. This led to new opportunities. Again, without the mainstream research I have already done in this area, I would not be equipped to make a contribution to this critical debate.

My faith very clearly influenced my work. First, I had to formulate models that were honest—models that would allow for both favorable and nonfavorable effects of trade on the environment. That was difficult to do since it would have been easier to set up a model that would give the answer I might want. Second, I put a priority on adopting policy choices that were best for not only preserving the environment but also best for the well-being of the poor. In other words, I tried to place my analysis in context. In thinking about environmental quality, I could not divorce it from the well-being of the poor or vice versa. Both are priorities for Christians, and my analysis had to preserve the importance of each objective. Third, I put a great deal of emphasis on the ability of individual countries to develop their own sets of environmental regulations, a policy unpopular in some circles. There is a great deal of "eco-imperialism" floating around. Countries with very stringent regulations are keen to impose their standards on other nations, and to use punitive measures when those standards are not accepted. Based on the Scriptures' concern for justice and dignity, as well as the economist's concern for efficiency, I had to speak out against this kind of policymaking.

With these examples, I hope to illustrate the need for Christians to be involved in mainstream economic research. Opportunities arise for them to make a difference in the outcomes of economic policy-making, by improving understanding of complex economic issues. If they are not doing mainstream research, they will be ill equipped to respond and will miss the opportunity to introduce a Christian voice into the debate.

A MODEL TO EMULATE

Let me end with an example to emulate. I am going to revisit the role of the research physician, only this time focusing on a real one. There is a Christian research physician who has modeled the kind of attitude towards mainstream work that I advocate here. In fact, C. Everett Koop has worn all three hats that I have described. Most people know his name, since he was the U.S. Surgeon General from 1981–1989. But some might not know that he is a professor of pediatric surgery, had spent a long time as a professor at the University of Pennsylvania, and was the editor of *The Journal of Pediatric Surgery.* One can see immediately that he has contributed to mainstream research in his field. In fact, he has also practiced the technical aspects of medicine, as a surgeon, using mainstream technical tools. He has won awards from many countries, including the highest honor from the Dominican Republic for his famous work separating conjoined twins. Koop has clearly worn the research physician's hat and the advocate's hat. But he has also worn the philosopher's hat. I have a book in my home library in which Koop and another Christian physician Timothy Johnson debate the ethics of critical health care issues such as abortion, AIDS, and euthanasia, and examine related policy from the standpoint of Christian ethics (Koop & Johnson, 1992). Not everyone can be a C. Everett Koop. I am certainly not one. But I think he is a good example of what it means to wear these three hats, and to be involved in mainstream research.

As I previously mentioned, this challenge is also a plea. Economics needs more Christians contributing to mainstream research. If Christians are willing to engage in it, they will help shape it—the issues addressed, the questions asked, and the solutions considered—with both transcendent and immanent criteria. Christians will then be ready to take up opportunities to bring healing and growth to the global economy.

Chapter 3

Market Behavior and Christian Behavior

Rebecca M. Blank

INTRODUCTION

The dominant tradition that economic behavior is motivated by rational self-interest is based on the notion that to be factual and predictive one must also be independent of any value position or normative judgment. Reliance on the narrow assumption of self-interested behavior, however, ignores the importance of certain rules of conduct that influence much of people's interactions with one another. To the extent that religious beliefs affect values and in turn the normative judgments on which policy is based, it is important that Christian economists participate in the policy-making process. The participation must go beyond mere commentary, incorporating the scholarly rigor expected by the mainstream of the discipline.

For many students, the first year of graduate school in economics is a time of total immersion in the subject. They live, eat, think, and breathe economics, spending long nights working on complex problems in economic theory. There is a purpose to this intense experience, however; at the end of the year, students come out thinking like an economist. If the training has been successful, they are not just able to analyze an economics problem in the appropriate way, but have developed an intuitive sense of what the right "economics answer" to a problem might be even before they confirm that with more formal analysis. They learn to look at the problems of the world through economics-tinted glasses, worrying about efficiency and incentive structure, and assuming that the people and institutions around them behave in accordance with the assumptions of the economic model.

I never felt that this immersion experience was as successful for me as for others. I came to realize that I viewed the world through a structure firmly established in my mind long before I started graduate work in economics, and not even that first year of "all economics, all the time" could dislodge it. More than 20 years of Sunday-school training, along with a heavy dose of social-action involvement, had left me with a perspective on individual and institutional behavior grounded in Christian theology. I never took the economic assumptions about individual behavior entirely seriously. I understood them to be a very useful model that could be used to analyze important economic questions. But I never made the mistake (at least as I defined it) of thinking that the economic model of behavior was a satisfying description of human activity. I knew it was at best a partial view of the world.

In this essay, I want to examine what economics teaches about behavior versus some of the core Christian teachings about behavior, and discuss where the two come together. My musings in this short essay are heavily based upon a much longer presentation published in the book *Is the Market Moral? A Dialogue on Religion, Economics, and Justice* (Blank & McGurn, 2003). I would encourage anyone with a deeper interest in this subject to consult that book, since in many places this essay provides only a short summary of topics discussed at greater length there.

THE ECONOMIC MODEL OF BEHAVIOR

This section provides a brief summary of issues that are taught in Economics 101 on most college campuses. The competitive market is at the core of mainstream economic thought, and when economists speak of "competitive markets" they have a very precise model in mind. The classic description of a competitive market is a spot-market, an auction market where everyone comes together and bargains out loud over prices and quantities. One can observe such a market at the Chicago Board of Trade, where traders yell back and forth and settle deals in the moment. But even those markets where transactions occur over time and across space have many of the elements that competitive markets describe.

The Benefits of the Competitive Model of Markets

The model of competitive markets that economists use is very powerful. From this model, one can predict how buyers and sellers are going to behave and the resulting price and quantity outcomes. Even more importantly, however, competitive markets result in some very real long-term economic benefits. First, a competitive market provides incentives for creativity and for entrepreneurship.

The competitive market rewards creative entrepreneurs who communicate more effectively why buyers should be interested in their product, produce a product that is higher quality, or develop a new product that people find useful or attractive.

Second, competitive markets foster efficiency. The more a firm can produce with a given set of resources—that is, the more efficient the production process—then the more advantageous is the firm's position within the market. A more efficient firm can underbid its competitors and capture more market share by selling an equally good product at a lower price. If competitors make management or production changes that increase efficiency, then the original firm will have to follow suit or lose customers. This drives market-wide efficiency improvements over time, so new technologies are rapidly adopted. One advantage of efficiency is lower prices for consumers.

Third, and very importantly, competitive markets require no central direction or organization. Market outcomes occur, to quote Adam Smith, "as by the workings of an invisible hand" ("The Wealth of Nations," 423). As a result, markets are associated with choices and the freedom of individuals to act in their own best interest without any intervening institutions. The market produces the goods that people want at a price they can afford, without anyone's oversight or direction.

Individual Behavior in a Competitive Market

In order for these benefits to occur, however, one must have a truly competitive market. This requires that individuals behave in particular ways when faced with economic decisions. Hence, the competitive model makes a variety of assumptions about how economic decision-making occurs in the market. Let me briefly lay out a few of the most important assumptions.

Individuals are assumed to always act to maximize their own self-interest. Individuals are assumed to know their preferences and to understand what will give them the most satisfaction. And it is assumed that they have the information they need in order to make choices that will maximize self-interest. For instance, as a buyer, I would maximize my self-interest by purchasing the services and goods that make me as well off as possible, conditional upon the income that I have available to spend. (In economics-speak, this is called "maximizing utility conditional upon income.") As a producer, I maximize my self-interest by maximizing profits subject to the production resources that I have available and the market demand for my product.

For many economic transactions, these are extremely reasonable assumptions. Assuming self-interested decision-making by a person who goes to the grocery store on Saturday morning is a fairly accurate assumption. That individual will decide whether to buy coffee based upon the price of the coffee, her own resources, and how much she likes it relative to the other things she can buy.

The basic model of economic decision-making also assumes that the key actor is the individual. Aggregate demand is nothing more than the aggregation of all individual decisions, each based on individual preferences. To predict the demand for coffee among my friends, I only have to know what each friend prefers in terms of her own coffee consumption. I can add up all the individual demands for coffee and figure out the group demand. Yet in the simple analysis, the group does not matter except as the sum of the parts; the list of other people who buy coffee is not going to affect any one person's demand for coffee. More sophisticated models can take account of "status goods," where one's own consumption of a good might increase if certain high-status people also buy it.

Finally, economists typically assume that better or worse can be measured by the metric of more or less: More choice is good. More goods are better than fewer goods. People's satisfaction is greater when they have more income and hence more choices about what they can purchase. There is an incentive for producers to utilize more efficient production processes because they allow one to produce *more* with a given set of resources.

Again, "more is better" is often an accurate assumption. For poor families, *more* may be the difference between health and hunger. For middle-income families, *more* may mean that a family vacation is affordable this year, allowing them to escape work and spend some time with the family. Or *more* may mean the ability to save enough for an adequate pension plan upon retirement.

Market Failure

If people do not behave the way the market assumes, then a competitive market does not exist and there is no guarantee that the benefits of competitive markets will occur. Let me suggest a few common ways in which "market failure" might occur; that is, situations where behavior does not proceed as assumed, and hence one cannot expect that the outcomes are efficient or desirable.

In competitive markets, people must have the information they need to make informed decisions. If people are misinformed, then there is no guarantee that a competitive market will produce efficient outcomes. For instance, if buyers know substantially less about a product than producers, producers can exploit this misinformation so buyers pay higher prices than they would if they actually understood what they were buying. Economists have written many books and articles about how lack of information, or information held by only a small number of people in the market, can distort prices and economic decisions.

Lack of full information is not the only situation leading to noncompetitive market outcomes. Bargaining between a buyer and seller leads to optimal outcomes only if those two individuals are the only ones who gain (or lose) from the sale. If there are benefits or costs to others, the buyers and sellers will pay no attention to this, and the price will not reflect those costs. This is a problem that economists refer to as an *externality*. The classic example of a negative externality is pollution. If a firm is spewing black smoke into the air while producing a product, everyone living nearby is negatively affected by it, but the people who buy the product ignore these effects. This means that the product sells at a lower price than it should (the cost of the pollution is not considered in the price); because the price is too low, more of it is bought and pollution is worse than it would be if pollution costs had been considered in the market sale.

An example of a good with a positive externality is basic education. It is not just the parent and the child who gain when the child learns how to read: the rest of society may benefit from having a literate citizenry. If these gains were ignored and education bought and sold on a private market, too few children would receive an education. School attendance is taken out of the market—public education is provided without charge, and attendance is mandated for all children—in order to avoid this problem.

There is a host of other ways in which markets may not meet the requirements of the competitive model. When market failures occur—when markets are not fully competitive—then often something can be done from outside groups (usually by government) to assure competitive markets. Hence, regulations that force full disclosure of product information or food contents are a way to avoid problems of misinformation. Regulations that require antipollution devices force firms to take account of the environmental costs of their production. Government services such as parks or highways provide public goods that benefit large numbers of people but cannot be bought readily through individual market transactions. One of the primary arguments for many types of government involvement in the economy is that such involvement works to enhance competition and to improve economic outcomes in situations of market failure.

Is This Model Too Simple?

What I have presented is the most basic economic model, taught in introductory economics classes everywhere. Yet, this is only a starting point. Economic theory is all about what happens in complex situations when markets do not at all resemble the simple model. Nobel Prizes in economics are not given to those who describe competitive markets, but to researchers who are working on complex economic situations of imperfect competition, or imperfect information; or situations where reputations are established over time and where history influences current decisions. Academic economists are well aware that the simple competitive model is too simple in many situations. Nonetheless, this simple model is an important model to understand. It is the null hypothesis in economic theory; when observing an economic outcome, the first question is typically, Is this the result of a competitive market? If the answer to that is no, then one must model where it diverges and how that affects the outcome.

The basic model of competitive markets is also a public icon. It is a reference point that is used not only within the economics profession but also much more broadly in public discussions about economic decision-making. Presentations about economic issues in the newspaper, or public discussions of economic activities, refer frequently to this basic competitive model.

In part, this is because this simple model has strong predictive abilities. Even with this model, one can make a good prediction about what will happen to price when demand falls; what will happen to wages when population grows; or how various government policies will affect economic outcomes. One reason why it is enjoyable to teach Economics 101 is that students can use this framework to understand the reasons for certain economic outcomes they have observed their entire lives.

For instance, using this basic model, if incomes go up I can predict that people will consume more, and I can even say something about what set of goods they are likely to buy more of and which goods they will buy less of. If taxes go up, I can say something about how consumer behavior will change and how savings will decline. If prices for one good go up, I can predict that people are going to switch to other substitute goods and can explain how they will make that decision.

For many of the readers of this essay, the examples given above are quite obvious. Of course people buy more when incomes rise; of course people save less when taxes rise. But this seems obvious only because the economic competitive model is deeply embedded in the culture and experience of those who grow up in market economies. Persons living in non-market economies would not necessarily find these behavioral responses self-evident.

As noted above, when markets fail—when the assumptions of the competitive model are not met—then there is a role for government. Within a market economy, however, government intervention is often viewed with some suspicion, seen as usable only in cases when market solutions are inadequate. An ongoing debate in the United States focuses on whether governmentally provided services could be better provided through the private sector: whether the U.S. Postal Service should be replaced with private mail service, or whether competition should be allowed for local schools. Among economists, there are deeply divided opinions about whether market failures are frequent or rare. Those who believe that the assumptions required for competitive markets are rarely met typically argue more strongly for greater government involvement in the economy.

Extending the Market Model into Other Areas

The market model is a description of how economic outcomes are determined. Within the industrialized world, however, where markets are pervasive, this model is often invoked in a wide variety of settings far outside of traditional economic decision-making. People talk about marriage markets and discuss marital decision-making in the same way as they discuss supermarket purchases; they refer to the political market for votes and discuss whether it is in the self-interest of a particular legislator to vote for or against a legislative proposal. The market model has come to be used not just for economic decisions, but as a generic model of how individuals make decisions. It is assumed that most decisions—both economic and noneconomic—are based on individualistic calculations of self-interest, with an individual weighing the benefits and costs.

Ann Landers's column was always one of my favorite parts of the newspaper. Women would regularly write to Ms. Landers and say, "This guy is cheating on me, and I don't know what to do. Should I leave him or should I stay?" Ann Landers had a classic reply. She would ask "Are you better off with him or without him?" An individual is asked to weigh her own self-interest and make a decision on the basis of the costs and benefits that she receives from marriage. It is a deeply economic model of decision making.

As the presumptions of market thinking come to dominate how people view a wide range of behaviors, grappling with limitations to the economic model of behavior is increasingly important. Particularly for people of faith, the economic model of behavior is at best incomplete. I turn now to a faith-based perspective on individual behavior and decision making.

CHRISTIAN TEACHING ON INDIVIDUAL BEHAVIOR

In this section I contrast some of the behavioral assumptions of competitive markets with some of the widely held Christian messages about what constitutes "right action." The assumptions of the economic model—self-interested behavior, individualistic decision-making and the presumption that more is better—must raise questions in the mind of any Christian. What does the Christian faith teach about appropriate behavior?

At the center of the Christian faith are love of God and faithfulness to God's calling. If God's love suffuses one's life, that love will spill out and manifest itself in behavior toward others. The United Church of Christ prints a bumper sticker which says "To love is to care; To care is to do." God's love in people's lives naturally leads them toward concern and care for others.

What Does the Christian Life Involve?

If God's love is a fundamental claim of the Christian faith, it suggests that there are some key theological elements missing from the market model of behavior. What follows is my list of at least a few important aspects of what I consider core elements of the Christian faith. Some might put these in a different order, or put a few other things on the list, but few Christians would disagree with these points.

First, Christian faith calls people into community with each other. One cannot be a Christian by oneself. The Biblical statement is very clear when Jesus says, "For where two or three are gathered in my name, I am there among them" (Matt 18:20). One's faith grows by interaction with the larger community of faith. Interactions between the self and the community are at the center of one's identity as a Christian.

Second, the Christian faith calls people to be other-interested as well as self-interested. Christianity validates the possibility of self-giving love. Christians' primary model for love is the love that they experience from God and a key demonstration of that love occurred in the sacrificial life and death of Jesus. As people experience God's love, they are called in turn to express that love in their own lives as they deal with others. I refer to this as other-interest.

The most immediate expression of other-interest reaches out to one's children, families, and perhaps close friends. But how far does faith require Christians to extend the concept of other-interest? Jesus says that the second great commandment is to love one's neighbor as oneself. The core question of the New Testament then becomes, Who is my neighbor and how do I express love to my neighbor? Loving one's neighbor clearly requires a genuine interest in his or her well-being. Other-interest sounds definably different than the self-interest discussed in economic models.

Third, the Christian faith affirms the abundant life measured not by the abundance of material goods but the abundance of the spirit. Again and again one learns from Biblical faith and from theological forebears that one is judged not by wealth but by faith. Those who focus on wealth are found wanting, "for one's life does not consist in the abundance of possessions" (Luke 12:15).

The Bible does not say that material life is unimportant. A central metaphor for Jesus' ministry to each Christian and to the church is the Eucharist, the sharing of food and drink. The communion service has deep spiritual meaning, but it is also directly connected to the reality of this world that requires the feeding of the body. There is a clear link in this ceremony between the material world and the spiritual world. Yet, the material world does not provide meaning in and of itself. Christians will be judged on faith and the uses to which they have put their wealth rather than the amount of their wealth. A key question is whether wealth is being used in a way that serves God.

Fourth, to a Christian choices are not morally neutral. Economics has a deep libertarian strain embedded in it, which claims that any choice made by a rational individual is acceptable. Within economics, my preferences are freely accepted, and there is no reason to judge them as better or worse than anyone else's. If I want to buy a good and if others want to be paid to produce it, then there should be a market for it, regardless of whether that good is food or pornography.

In contrast, Christian faith claims that there is a moral valuation associated with choice. Indeed, some choices are better than others. One's choices should be evaluated on the basis of whether they turn one towards God. In making decisions, Christians must ask the questions, Do these choices reflect my faith? Do they express God's love in my life?

Of course, this moral valuation of choice leads to very, very deep divisions and arguments within Christianity. Is abortion a choice that turns one away from God? Or, are there circumstances under which abortion is a better choice than other alternatives? Christians argue about this issue because they believe that choices are not morally neutral. They care about the social and moral implications of choices that they believe pull people further away from God.

Finally, Christian faith demands that Christians be concerned for the poor and those in need. The U.S. Catholic bishops (1986) discuss the special obligation of Christians to respond to poverty and to economic need. The liberation theologians claim that God is with the poor in their struggle, and that to be faithful to God one must also be present in that same struggle (Cone, 1997). Throughout the Old Testament, the prophetic writings, and the New Testament, a concern for those in need is stated again and again. Widows and orphans receive particular attention in God's concern. Indeed, responding to the needs of the poor is a way to demonstrate directly one's Christian faith. When speaking about feeding the hungry and clothing the naked, Jesus is clear: "Truly I tell you, just as you did not do it to one of the least of these, you did not do it to me" (Matt 25:45).

Is Other-Interest a Useful Concept?

In a modern market economy, how do Christians reconcile these Christian tenets with the self-interested economic behavior that is typically assumed? Let me focus here on the concept of other-interested love. I take other-interest as a counterpoint to self-interest. It suggests a situation in which the needs and preferences of another person are taken more seriously than one's own needs and preferences. One makes certain choices because it will increase the satisfaction of another, even though there may be a real cost to oneself.

Let me describe an example that clearly contrasts other-interest and self-interest. Think about two couples. In one relationship both individuals are purely self-interested. They live together, but each takes care of only herself or himself. Each person's needs are met because each is completely self-interested. In another relationship, both are other-interested. In expressing love to each other, each of them puts the needs of the other person before their own. Each person's needs are met because each is cared for by the other. The outcome may be quite similar in both cases, but the underlying motivations and behaviors are quite different.

This suggests that in a tight community where *somebody* takes each person's interests seriously and responds to them, other-interested behavior might result in aggregate outcomes not very different from self-interested behavior. In practice, tightly knit communities in which other-interest dominates are unlikely to occur outside of very small groupings such as marriage, larger kinship groups, or small homogeneous communities. In most cases, one needs to think about the possibility for situations in which other-interest and self-interest exist alongside each other. Indeed, there is no reason why other-interested love should imply a lack of self-interest. Persons who lack any degree of self-regard and self-interest are often unable to effectively respond to others. Jesus asks that Christians love their neighbors as they love themselves (Mark 12:31). He does not ask them to love only their neighbor without loving themselves.

Other-interested behavior can lead toward quite different outcomes than self-interested behavior. For instance, other-interested behavior may lead one to engage in very inefficient behavior that does not produce obvious results or positive outcomes. An adult child may spend hours sitting by the bed of an unconscious parent who has no idea that she is there. A person may spend hours listening one more time to the complaints of his friend while knowing that none of those complaints are going to change. Listening expresses caring; in fact, by using one's time inefficiently—by being willing to listen again and again to the same litany of complaints—one might be validating the importance of the other person. Similarly, parents engage endlessly with their two-year-old, reading a silly book for the 150th time.

From an economic point of view, these may all be very inefficient ways to spend one's time. But they demonstrate other-interested love, where one's actions exemplify concern and love for the other person rather than one's own self-interest. Stanley Hauwerwas (2001) has a footnote in one of his books that notes the inefficiency of Mother Teresa caring for the dying rather than feeding hungry children, implicitly claiming that a cost-benefit calculation would not be likely to support this action.

I suspect most of us would agree that other-interested behavior is surely possible, at least occasionally, and particularly in our relationships with family and close friends. The interesting question is, Is this a useful concept in a market economy, in economic relationships that occur outside the realm of close family and friends? Other-regarding behavior expressed outside of one's immediate circle of family and friends is a strange concept in modern U.S. culture. It is a concept about which one might even be suspicious. It may sound cultic to proclaim that one cares about other people, and particularly people that one may not know very well.

The Challenge of Other-Interest in a Global Economy

Can one can consistently show other-interest and love outside of an immediate set of family and friends? Let me first say more about the problem of other-interest in an impersonal market and then suggest some possibilities for how this might occur.

The economic choices made in the market often seem completely separated from personal relationships. For instance, if I walk to the corner and buy a newspaper, I might smile at the person who sells it to me, but I have no other relationship with that individual. Or, if I go to the store and buy groceries, I typically assume that I have no previous or future relationship with the lady at the checkout counter, much less with the individuals who made and packaged that food. When goods sold locally are produced thousands of miles away, it eliminates the personal connection with the people who produced those goods.

This is a significant shift from the traditional agrarian economy, in which local communities were often largely self-sufficient. Neighbors were the primary source of trade and economic exchange. People were connected with their entire economic network; indeed, economic transactions were often based more on kinship relationships and geographical proximity than on self-interest or preference.

In contrast, when individuals find themselves in a global market economy, there are far fewer networks of personal connection with any of the other persons who make or sell goods. This makes self-interested behavior much easier to pursue, and under these circumstances the economic model of behavior is likely to be an effective predictor of behavior.

This global economy has clear benefits that accrue to all who participate in it. People are not constrained to only buy those products that they or their immediate neighbors can produce, as is true in a subsistence agrarian economy. Because products are produced in locations where the necessary materials and skills are most available, prices are often substantially lower than in more closed economies without international trade. This benefits most consumers, and the lower prices may particularly benefit low-income families.

In short, it is not by chance that Wal-Mart has become the largest company in America and that other large-scale retail chains have grown as well. Wal-Mart offers an enormous range of products from all over the world at very low prices. People like choice, they like seeing more goods, they like low prices, and hence they go to Wal-Mart. In contrast, the local corner store is typically more expensive and has more limited choices.

But this does pose a very difficult question: How does one demonstrate other-interest within this global network of narrow relationships, where there are few face-to-face interactions and often limited information about the people who make the product that is being bought? The irony is that on the one hand, the global marketplace reemphasizes one's connection to the rest of the world. It makes the answer to Who is my neighbor? all the clearer: Your neighbor is more than the person who sits next to you on the bus to work. Your neighbors include the people in China producing the clothes you wear and also the people in Mexico or California who harvest and process the food you eat. By buying what they make, your life is connected with these people in a very real sense. One's connection with people across the globe has expanded because of this global economy.

On the other hand, one's ability to respond in any personal way to these faraway neighbors is more limited than the ability to respond to geographical neighbors. As communities widen, contact becomes limited to the narrow economic relationships of self-interested buying and selling.

LIVING IN FAITH AND LIVING IN THE MARKET

Many have responded to the growing global economy by drawing a distinction between the public and private spheres. This means claiming that other-interest is not really relevant for economic transactions in the global economy, but is only relevant within the private world of family and friends. They argue that one's first responsibility as a Christian is to express love to one's family and immediate friends and to get those relationships right. In contrast, the public sphere is run by different rules, and one must participate in the economic system on its own terms. The economic realm interacts with that part of people's lives that is defined by self-interest and individual decision-making. The private realm involves family and friends, and in this realm each is responsible for establishing loving and other-interested relationships.

Expressing other-interest and community concern toward family and close communities of friends is surely a faithful response. For some individuals whose resources and energy are limited or whose childrearing or family-support responsibilities take all of their time and energy, it may be the only humanly possible response. For many individuals, however, especially those who enjoy leisure time and excess wealth (that is, for many Americans), I do not find this to be a fully satisfying nor faithful response. It is difficult to believe that the call to other-interest does not include neighbors with whom Christians interact daily through their economic lives. How have different people found ways to express other-interest to neighbors within a global economic community? There are a variety of different responses. Let me just mention a few.

One option is to withdraw from at least some aspects of the global marketplace. For instance, there are those who focus on growing their own food, or buying from local cooperatives. Others elect lives of voluntary simplicity, in which they refuse to participate in some parts of the global economy such as mass media, or luxury goods, or excessive consumption. For instance, Berry (1987) writes about this option. He argues that we should return to a neighborhood-based system of production. The price may be a lack of strawberries in January, or higher prices for some goods that are more expensive to produce nearby. In return, however, one gains a personal connection to the people who make the products one buys, or a personal connection to those who buy the products one sells.

For many, substantial withdrawal from the global marketplace is extremely difficult. In my mind, the interesting challenge is to find ways to live faithfully within the global marketplace. Some do this by focusing on one or two issues, informing themselves about these issues more globally, and acting as advocates. In this case, one might pay attention to some key companies and how they are behaving with regard to workers' rights or environmental usage. A variety of advocacy networks have sprung up to support just this type of activism, often focused on a variety of justice-based concerns such as farm-worker rights, rainforest preservation, or sweatshop operations. Focusing on a selected set of issues recognizes that people are humanly limited and cannot deal with all problems facing all people. By trying to work on some problems facing some people, however, one can take on responsibility toward faraway neighbors and demonstrate other-interest.

Another response is to express concern and other-interest within the communities where one is personally present and involved. This might mean treating with the utmost dignity and respect any individual with whom one interacts, whether the flight attendant on the airplane, the vendor at the corner newspaper stand, or the person working in another division of the same company. It might mean working at the local food pantry, tutoring children in the schools, or being a special friend to a family in crisis in the local church. If everyone treats nearby neighbors with concern and attention, it may be less important for anyone to be concerned about those further away. In this case, each community holds primary responsibility for those who live within it. Of course, some communities may not be defined by geography but by other connections. For instance, those who work inside international corporations may have a responsibility to that community that explicitly includes the well-being of workers who are hired in Third World countries.

A final way to respond is to work with organizations that have the capacity to respond to economic problems more broadly than any single individual. The demands of faith may require not just an individual response to the problem of helping one's neighbor, but a collective response. I want to say a bit more about this option. Collective action as groups of individuals or through established institutions (governmental or church-based or other nonprofits) can provide a mechanism through which individuals can participate with others to respond to neighbors nearby and far away.

There are two types of collective organizations for consideration. First, there are governmental organizations that link people nationally and often around the globe. (This is particularly true for Americans, given the size and dominance of the United States in world diplomacy and international economic structures.) Government action reflects national concerns, and it is entirely valid to demand that one's government be involved with issues of human rights. Hence, one way to show other-interest is to be active citizens, demanding that elected officials give priority to operating effective schools in low-income neighborhoods or lobbying for foreign aid that encourages economic development in poor countries. Increasingly, international organizations, such as the United Nations and its subsidiary organizations, play a key role in food relief, immigrant resettlement, and cross-boundary disputes. Other-interest may involve direct support given to some of these efforts, or organized action within one's own country to assure that national and international outreach efforts work effectively.

Second, faith-based and other nonprofit organizations act as outreach and service organizationsto connect people worldwide. Organizations such as Catholic Charities, Lutheran World Relief, or Heifer Project provide direct services supported by local churches and their members. Other organizations such as the Red Cross, or Oxfam, or Big Brothers/Big Sisters are less directly church-supported or organized but provide a similar institutional outlet to organize and focus individual efforts to assist neighbors both nearby and faraway. Support or involvement in civic and private organizations can connect Christians individually to people across the globe, even within a modern global and impersonal economy.

In a more global economy, if they are to demonstrate other-interest Christians must often rely on institutional activities that go beyond anything that they as individuals can organize on their own. From a Christian perspective, I consider that one of the government's most important roles is to provide the opportunity for collective outreach and action by a civic community.

The Role of the Church

The church as an institution has an important role to play in all of this as well. The church needs to teach and preach about the value of community service, other-interest, and spiritual (rather than consumer) abundance in individual lives, topics not well articulated in a world that relies too much on individualistic, self-interested models of decision making.

The role of the church is not to be antimarket or promarket, but to be life-affirming. That means that its role is necessarily different in different societies and at different points in time. In more traditional societies, the role of the church may well be to speak about the dangers of corruption and about the advantages of opening up of market opportunities to a wider variety of citizens. In modern American society, where cultural norms reinforce the economic model's valuation of self-interest, individualism, and consumerism, the role of the church must be to affirm values that the market does not.

The church should act to educate its members about the importance of balancing self-interest and other-interest, individual concerns with community concerns, and the church as an institution should provide opportunities to its members actively to live out these other values not just in their family lives but in their public and economic lives as well. The church should help individuals think about how faith and economics come together and should provide a public language different from the language of the market.

FINAL COMMENTS

One of the questions I have been asked by some of my activist Christian friends (often in slightly incredulous voice) is, How can you possibly be both a believer in market economics and a Christian at the same time? There is a radical and a prophetic tradition within the church that answers You can't. This is an entirely valid response out of certain faith traditions. Individuals may feel called to withdraw from the market and from market society and move toward a simpler lifestyle. Or individuals may feel called to work on transforming markets and transforming society in some way that produces a better and more just economy than any that economists can visualize or implement today.

I do not speak from that prophetic tradition. Asking how one can participate in global markets and still be a Christian is, to my mind, a bit like asking, Given the sinfulness of human beings, can one be both Christian and human at the same time? The answer is, Of course you can be both. For the Christian, to be human is to be both.

Similarly, to be human in the twenty-first century United States is to live in the midst of a global market economy. This creates a need for Christians to find ways to integrate their faith concerns and their economic lives. Christians are called into an ongoing tension between living in this world and not being entirely of it. Christians must live between what God wants of their lives and what they make of their lives. Interaction with a market economy must have this same balance between acceptance and rejection.

Outcomes in the market are rarely *either* good or bad. They are more frequently *both* good and bad. Markets enrich the lives of some who were previously poor, while excluding others; they generate new jobs and encourage the development of new human talents, even while they displace or disemploy others whose skills are no longer as useful.

Christianity does not call its followers to turn their backs on the market economy and on the good—or the bad—that it can do. But Christian faith does remind believers that their talents are not entirely of their own making. It does not advocate overvaluing the things of this world nor turning towards greed, but using economic capacity in ways that serve God and one's neighbors as well as oneself. Faith asserts that wealth is not an end in itself, but a means that can be used to improve the well-being of individuals and their neighbors. Wealth can generate jobs and lessen poverty; it can provide valued goods to the community such as better schools or more parks.

There is no need to choose between participating in a market economy and being a Christian. Rather, Christians need to find ways to live in the market but not be wholly possessed by it, recognizing that different people will find the appropriate balance at different points on the spectrum. The challenge for Christians is to discern the meaning of faithful action within a modern economy.

Economists face policy challenges all around them. Issues concerning the human condition beg for the economic perspective. Likewise, the same issues can benefit from insights gained from faith perspectives. Christians have no choice but to use their economic knowledge, influenced by Christian values, to address the problems that challenge modern people individually and collectively.

Chapter 4

The Economics of Racial Equality and Justice

Glenn C. Loury

INTRODUCTION

It is essential that Christian scholars, particularly economists, speak out on the important social issues that plague society. Fulfilling the advocacy role in public policy requires that Christians confront from a Christian perspective critical issues that affect people individually and collectively. If Christians focus on incentives and efficiency alone, they neglect the contribution that their spiritual identity provides to the discussion.

I am a Christian and an economist. How, one might ask, do those distinct aspects of a scholar's identity relate to one another? In my own case, I became an economist many years before I became a Christian, so my methodological commitments—my "school of thought" commitments, so to speak—were forged long before I began to raise questions about how my work might be connected to my faith. Yet, since becoming a Christian my practice of economics has changed, and the work I will discuss here gives evidence of these changes. I have found it instructive to reflect upon this transformation, and I wish to begin this essay by sharing a bit of that reflection.

Economists study markets, the behavior of consumers and firms, the art and science of buying and selling, and the theory of rational choice. This is important work, to be sure. It is, for example, prudent to think carefully about incentives when creating social programs. Economists should try to conceptualize and to measure the costs and benefits of alternative public policies. Such an approach is a technical enterprise with respect to which economics has considerable power. Even so, as a Christian I do not consider this analytical perspective, by itself, adequate to the task of social prescription. Indeed, the single-minded focus on benefits and costs that one associates with economic science can be a profoundly impoverished way of thinking about how people should live together in society.

Let me give an example drawn from recent discussions about the problem of racial profiling. There is an obvious cost–benefit perspective on that problem: When screening resources are limited, there is a statistical argument that an agent seeking to detect an unobserved hazard can do so more efficiently by making use of any readily observable information that correlates with the presence of the hazard. If one happens to know that dangerous people are drawn disproportionately from a group whose members look a certain way, then using that knowledge in the design of a screening process will, as a statistical matter, ease the monitoring problem. Economists will see immediately just how such an analysis would proceed. On the other hand, when people undertake to classify others categorically, and to treat them differently based on this categorization, they do more than simply solve a resource-allocation problem. They also make a statement about how people are to look upon and relate to one another. Often, it seems to me, this expressive aspect of policy (i.e., whether or not one wants to make such a statement) is nearly the whole ball game.

Put differently, the determination of how people ought to relate to one another can be a more fundamental judgment than is an efficiency calculation of the costs and benefits associated with alternative courses of action. And yet, whereas the principles entailed by a cost–benefit calculation are easy to discern (e.g., more is better than less), to what principles can people look for guidance on the question of how they ought to look upon people different from themselves? Thus, and notwithstanding its statistical benefits, a case against racial profiling might be made along the following lines: When racial categorization is built into the bureaucratic practice of law enforcement or antiterrorism defense, it thereby gives a face to the enemy, saying in effect that the enemy, those rightly feared and despised, look more or less like this. When this face of the enemy is also the face of a great many of one's neighbors and friends, pursuit of efficiency through profiling has the effect of sundering the community and debasing its values. Now, does it make any sense to talk of the benefits and the costs of doing, or not doing, something like that? I think not. Because value commitments (What manner of people are we, and how then must we comport ourselves?) can transcend economic concerns (How much do we have, and how might we get even more?), people are thankfully often moved to eschew what would otherwise appear to be the most efficient course of action. As a result, the cost–benefit calculus is, in general, insufficient to prescribe a course of action.

Now a critic will come along and say, Ah, but you have simply failed fully to account for all of the cost and benefits. Doing so would permit one to include value commitments within a cost–benefit framework. I understand this argument, but think that occasions will arise where, in the nature of the case, it is impossible in principle to do such a modified accounting. For I am talking here about the beliefs people hold and the ideals they are prepared to affirm. It seems to me that matters such as these transcend, cannot be ignored, and are incommensurate with the kinds of costs and benefits that are an economist's concern. Consider a person tempted to steal some item but who, in the end, decides not to. Contrast two modes of reasoning that can support this decision not to steal: The person calculates that to risk detection and punishment entails costs that exceed the benefits of acquiring the item. Alternatively, the person says to himself or herself, with conviction, I am not a thief, and I must comport myself accordingly. My point here is that an analyst ought not try to assimilate the second mode of reasoning to the first by introducing the fictitious notion of a "cost to thinking of oneself as a thief." To do so is to compare apples to oranges by asking, in effect, What is this person's "willingness to pay" for an unsullied self-concept?

More generally, I am of the view that social science can capture only a part of the human subject. Of necessity, its methods project the full person onto those material and deterministic dimensions that scholars think they understand. As an object of scientific inquiry, the human subject must ultimately be reduced to a mechanism. Yet, in so doing social scientists leave out that which most makes a person human. They leave out the soul. As a believer, my fundamental conviction is that human beings are not defined by desires. Indeed, I would even deny that they are defined by their biological inheritance. God is not finished with us when he deals us our genetic hand. As spiritual beings, what people are in the fullness of their humanity transcends that which can be grasped with the particular vision that an economist, a sociologist, or psychologist might bring.

Consider some examples: What incentive scheme devised by an economist could ever be as effective in prompting the dedicated, disciplined, systematic involvement of parents in their children's lives, as would be the promptings of conscience that come to parents when they think of themselves as God's stewards in the lives of their children? To distinguish between these two methods of motivating parents is to do more than simply identify distinct points on a spectrum of instrumentality, with one modality of intervention being more efficient than another. Rather, these are qualitatively different ways of approaching the problem—one involving self-serving motivation rooted in maximizing behavior by parents, the other entailing the parents' self-understandings, which understandings devolve from their more fundamental convictions about who they are, who made them, and what obligations follow in light of their certain knowledge of who and whose they are.

Questions of incentives and efficiency are of a fundamentally different, lower order than questions of spiritual identity concerning "who and whose we are"—which is not to say that the former questions are unimportant. I wish to stress that, in this assertion of the limits of a cost–benefit calculus, I do not repudiate the life of the mind. I simply claim that to grasp fully the nature of human subjects, social scientists must reckon with this transcendent dimension. I am arguing against arrogance, not against the use of intellect. What I reject is the presumption that intellect on its own can do what it plainly cannot do—tell people the meaning of their lives. Economics cannot finally resolve the most profound questions at the center of people's struggles as individuals, as families, and as a nation: Who are we? What must we do? How shall we live? What is right? When all the statistical analyses have been rendered, people still have to step back and ask such questions. And, absent the spiritual grounding that permits individuals meaningfully to pose such questions, intellectual efforts amount to so much puzzle solving, an activity that in the end has no life.

Permit me to give another illustration. Some years ago I taught at Harvard's John F. Kennedy School of Government, in an ethics course for the public policy program. The students were all smart, ambitious, committed, preparing to run the world. I and my fellow professors mounted a mandatory one-semester course in ethics, leading students through the discussion of hard cases and studying with them, among other things, relevant philosophical literature. The course enrollment was so large that ten faculty members were required to teach all of the sections. One would lecture to the full class every week, and the professors met regularly to coordinate activities.

At one such meeting I said to my colleagues, in effect: "Okay, so we have now covered Kant and Rawls, we have read the reflections of thoughtful public officials who have considered the ethical dilemmas of governance, and so forth. That is all very good and very useful. And yet when crunch time comes, and our students have to make an ethically crucial decision, knowing what is right will be the least of their problems. Doing what is right will be the key difficulty, and that is not mainly an intellectual issue. Where will our students find the resources to do what they know to be right when crunch time comes?" Now of course, in such a secular environment I did not mean that we should direct our students to accept Jesus Christ as Lord and Savior. I did not mean to say, Just take Jesus on board and all will be well. But the fact was that many students came to the course with spiritual commitments of their own. Why not remind them of those commitments and urge them, in accordance with their respective traditions, to be mindful of the spiritual component to the problems that they were learning about? Certainly, despite the university's secularity, the professors could incorporate this consideration into their own pedagogy. To do so would have been to adopt a richer and more humane model of the students—seeing them as something more than mere calculating machines.

Here is a final example. Social scientists have argued that a disadvantaged background can irreversibly impair a child's development. Much evidence confirms that early-life social disadvantage of one kind or another correlates with the extent of later-life problems. But whatever the nature of such environmental influences, there are people in poor communities working with children who have been scarred by all manner of disadvantage. These people often succeed in their attempts to reach into the lives of these children, to form relationships with them, to create institutions devoted to serving them, and thereby to mitigate the harm associated with social deprivation. Religious congregations in inner-city communities, for instance, are working with troubled youngsters and, with God's help, are changing lives. Their efforts fly in the face of a deterministic developmental psychology that says if the youngster is exposed to certain influences then the adult will be inclined to behave in a certain way. Now of course, one can study these faith-based interventions as a technical problem—asking, for example, under what conditions the religion-inspired programs work well. One would certainly want to do so before making any broad claims about their effectiveness. But what interests me most about this example is its antideterministic character. Social science tends to offer deterministic accounts of human action, with randomness introduced mainly to account for the errors in human observations. Its theories say, in effect, that material conditions mediated by social institutions cause people to behave in a certain way. Yet it may be more plausible to think of material and institutional expectations as establishing only a fairly wide range within which behavior must lie, with the specific behavior within this range for any particular person being dependent upon factors of motivation, will, and spirit—factors having to do with what that person takes to be the source of meaning in his or her life, with what animates him or her at the deepest level.

If this is right, then it is crucial to grasp the implication that the behavior of freely choosing, socially situated, spiritually endowed human beings will in some essential way be indeterminate, unpredictable, and even mysterious. For when the exercise of human agency is driven by what people understand to be meaningful—by what they believe in—then the intersubjective processes of social interaction and mutual stimulation that generate and sustain patterns of belief in human communities become centrally important. But these processes of persuasion, conformity, conversion, myth construction and the like are open-ended. They are at best only weakly constrained by material conditions. That is, while what people believe about the transcendent powerfully shapes how they act in a given situation, these beliefs cannot themselves be deduced as a necessary consequence of people's situations. One can always agree to believe differently or more fervently, particularly if those with whom one is closely connected are undergoing a similar transformation. Religious revivals and reformations can sweep through ranks and change collective views of the world virtually overnight. people can be moved to make enormous sacrifices on behalf of abstract goals. Humans are ever capable—as the Czech playwright-turned-politician, Vaclav Havel, has said so well—of "transcending the world of existences."

Now I admit to being deeply moved by the fact that humans are spiritual creatures, generators of meaning, beings that must not and cannot live by bread alone. I have seen the power for good and for ill of communal organization acting through the constitution of collectivities that are like-minded in their understandings about the meaning of life, about "what God has put us here for." My conviction, as a Christian who happens also to be an economist, is that until economic science takes this aspect of the human drama with the utmost seriousness economics will do justice neither to the subject of its study, nor to the national communities that look to it for useful advice about a host of social ills.

OBSERVATIONS ON *THE ANATOMY OF RACIAL INEQUALITY*

I turn now to a discussion of my book, *The Anatomy of Racial Inequality* (2002). My faith commitments as a Christian have influenced the work that leads up to that book. The core motivation for the argument of the book lies in the distinction between viewing the problem of racial inequality in *transactional* terms, versus viewing it in *relational* terms. I see this distinction between relations and transactions as a spiritual matter. The most influential text in economics on the subject of discrimination is still Gary Becker's work from the 1950s, *The Economics of Discrimination* (1971). The problem Becker posed in his book concerns the implications for a market economy of the fact that people have preferences leading them to avoid trading with certain others. The existence of these preferences together with some accounting of how markets work allows an analyst to deduce the implications of this "taste for discrimination" in regard to, for instance, racial disparities in employment and wages. Now, a standard criticism of Becker's argument—an argument, I might add, that has been very fruitful and very important in the history of economic research on this topic—is that it begs the question of from whence such preferences derive in the first place. Why do these preferences exist?

Of course, that question comes up everywhere in economics. It strikes me, however, as a particularly crucial question for the problem of racial inequality because, as I hinted in the earlier discussion of racial profiling, such "preferences" constitute an expression of who some human beings understand other human beings to be—of how they see themselves in relation to the other. When one speaks about race in the United States, there is a history to consider. This history is not merely a source of moral authority for the victimized: "Oh, look what happened in the past. It was awful and something is now owed." Rather, I would argue that this history is a place where one might examine race by looking for some understanding of the mental maps inside the heads of people who deal with one another now. If economists speak only about transactions, if they envision only a host of autonomous individuals interacting with one another in pursuit of their own gain, then, as important as such considerations might be, they may fail to ask what some people in society understand the marks on the bodies of other human beings to mean. How, one ought to ask, do people understand themselves and why do they identify in a particular way? Why do they erect and affirm social boundaries along these racial dimensions and not some others? Those are relational questions.

I can express this difference between a transactional and a relational approach in another way: Economists see inequality. They ask themselves about people's rights. People have a right not to be discriminated against, they say. People have a right, if they can pay, to be able to buy; if they have goods of comparable quality to those of another person, they ought to be able to sell without being differentially treated. Now whether or not I would call this a *right,* I do have some sympathy for the position that asserts people ought not to be discriminated against in the marketplace. But there are huge realms of social behavior in which I would not so readily embrace the view that it is wrong for people to be discriminated against. In the sphere of private social intercourses—when people decide whom to marry, where to worship, where to live, with whom to send their children to school and so forth—when people make decisions about association and the connection with others, they are then exercising their right to personal autonomy. They may well decide to do so in a racially discriminatory fashion. And I cannot see any justification for those kinds of discriminatory decisions to be coercively overridden by a state committed to equality. Because when people elect in private social intercourse to associate with one another, partly on racial terms, they exercise an autonomy that is an essential part of themselves.

Let me not be obscure. What I am saying here is that racially assortative mating is deeply rooted in American society. People do not come together randomly across the lines. The continued existence of racial categories as sociologically meaningful distinctions in society depends upon this assortative mating. For in its absence, the physical differences associated with racial groups (differences of morphology, of skin color, of hair texture) could not be sustained across the generations. A sufficiently high degree of cross-boundary marriage and reproduction would, in due course, spell the certain end of racial categorization. Nevertheless, I know nobody who holds that persons are entitled to racially unbiased treatment in the marriage market—that it is unfair racial discrimination if an individual belonging to group A prefers to marry someone who also belongs to group A. People may have views about this in their own private lives, but I know no one who would publicly take the position that this is something in which the state has an interest—something the Fourteenth Amendment addresses. Yet the reality that people relate to each other in this way (exercising racial discrimination in choice of mates) is profoundly significant for the perpetuation across generations of racial identity and racial inequality. So to understand the inequality problem, it is important to think about the relational as well as the transactional aspect.

In what follows, I will briefly discuss some of the ideas in my book, and then reflect a bit on how I was influenced by my Christian faith in the writing of this book. My book is aimed at asking and sketching answers to three questions: What is race? Why is racial inequality so stubbornly persistent in American society? And in what does racial justice consist?

What is race? My answer: Race is *embodied social signification.* My theory of race comes down to the bumper sticker, "race = embodied social signification." I am going to unpack that phrase and explain just what I mean.

Why is racial inequality so stubbornly persistent? My answer: Racial inequality is so stubbornly persistence in American society in part because of the problem of *biased social cognition.* In due course I will expand on my second bumper-sticker phrase, biased social cognition.

In what does racial justice consist? Well, that big question implicitly begs another one: Is there any such thing as racial justice? I am presuming that there is. And my answer to the first question is that the distinction between blindness and neutrality is central to getting a handle on how to think about racial justice. Racial *blindness* has to do with rules of public action—e.g., whether the University of Texas uses information about an applicant's race when deciding whom to admit. Racial *neutrality* has to do with the goals or purposes of public action—whether or not the intention to mitigate or ameliorate racial inequality is a desirable public end. Judgments about the desirability of alternative distributions of well-being among members of the racial groups are judgments about neutrality. Judgments about whether the rules of public action rely on racial information are judgments about blindness. This distinction, I hold, is central to any reflection on the problem of racial justice. There are, to be sure, many other things addressed in the book, but those are the three central matters, which I will now discuss in more detail.

What Is Race?

Any theory of race, it seems to me, must explain the fact that people take note of and assign significance to superficial markings on the bodies of other human beings—their skin color, hair texture, facial bone structure, and other physical characteristics. This practice is virtually universal in human societies. Scientists have conjectured that it has a deep neurological foundation. So this is the point of departure for my analysis. I refer to a society as being "raced" when its members routinely partition into groups the field of human subjects whom they encounter in that society, and when this sorting convention is based on the subjects' possession of some cluster of observable bodily marks. This leads to my claim that, at bottom, race is all about embodied social signification.

Let us call this the social–cognitive approach to thinking about race. It may be usefully contrasted with an approach derived from the science and art of biological taxonomy. There one endeavors to classify human beings on the basis of natural variation in genetic endowments across geographically isolated subpopulations. Such isolation was a feature of the human condition until quite recently (on an evolutionary time scale), and it permitted some independence of biological development within subpopulations, which can be thought to have led to the emergence of distinct races. When social critics deny the reality of race, they have in mind this biological–taxonomic notion, and what they deny is that meaningful distinctions among contemporary human subgroups can be derived in this way. Whether they are right or not would appear to be a scientific question. But whatever the merits of this dispute, it is important to understand that the validity of racial classification as an exercise in biological taxonomy is distinct conceptually from the validity and relevance of my concern with racial categorization as an exercise in social–cognition.

Moreover, and this too is absolutely critical, to establish the scientific invalidity of racial taxonomy demonstrates neither the irrationality nor the immorality of adhering to a social convention of racial classification. Even if race is not a useful biological–taxonomic category, it does not follow from this that seeing oneself or other people as belonging to races is akin to belief in witches—that is, to crediting as real a thing that does not exist. I adopt the linguistic convention that, when saying "person A belongs to race X," I mean "person A has physical traits that (in a given society, at a fixed point in history, under the conventions of racial classification extant there and then) will cause him to be classified (by a preponderance of those he encounters in that society or by himself) as belonging to race X." And whereas this maneuver would seem deeply unsatisfactory if applied to the question of someone being a witch (saying "she is a witch" if enough people think she is), I think this is a plausible way to proceed when discussing the social reality of race. This is a pragmatic judgment on my part, not an a priori logical claim. That is, I hold this view because the social convention of thinking about other people, and about oneself as belonging to different races is so longstanding and deeply ingrained in American political culture that it has taken on a life of its own. Belief in witchcraft (in this society, at this juncture in history) has no comparable salience. If it did, then the reality of that belief and of the practice of classifying people on that basis would be of interest, regardless of its objective correctness. Thus, for students of the history and political economy of the modern multiracial nation state, the logical exercise of deconstructing racial categories by trying to show that nothing real lies behind them is largely beside the point.

This point of view is supported by the theory of "self-confirming stereotypes" that I advance in the book. Suppose I am to have some repairs done on my home. I hire workmen, some of whom are Jamaican and some Chinese. Imagine that the Jamaicans are very punctual, effective, and cheap, while the Chinese tend to come late, do a poor job, and overcharge. (If you are offended by this supposition, you can reverse the characterizations of the groups!) My point is that I will notice any such average difference, and I may well assimilate this knowledge by associating disparities in average worker performance with characteristics of the groups. To do so would merely be to engage in the efficient cognitive processing of social information. This is just what I observed earlier about racial profiling. In the example at hand, I might be inclined to profile these workmen, to make generalizations about their racial or ethnic groups. In this way, race—marks on human bodies—can become socially significant. The marks become "hooks" on which people hang their expectations, or "bins" in which people store their experiences before forming the historical averages they use to estimate the likelihood of various future events and, by so doing, to get some informational purchase on their environment.

Race can be informative in that way, and it is not hard to think of examples where the logic of self-interest reinforces and confirms this general tendency. I give an example in my book involving taxicabs. Just imagine for a moment that there are two groups of people—young black men and older white women, let us say. Based on appearance, members of these two groups are easily distinguished at a glance on the streets by anyone driving a taxi. Let us further suppose that, on the average, the likelihood of robbery as perceived by the taxi drivers is higher when passengers are young black men than when passengers are older white women.

Under such conditions, a taxicab driver might be reluctant to stop for young black men. If most drivers share this perception, a young black man would expect to wait a long time to get a taxi. That raises the effective price of taxicab services to such people, since the full cost involves both time and money. Now, consider the elasticity of demand for services among two types of young black men—those intent on robbery and those not. I posit that, compared to the law-abiding, those who want to rob taxis will have a relatively inelastic demand for taxi services: They only need one taxi to stop in order to get in their night's work! So, even if taxis are slow to stop for them, they will not be much discouraged from hailing taxis. But the law-abiding, when confronted by the prospect of a long wait for taxi services, might be expected to avail themselves of the next best alternative—to bring their own car, take public transportation, carpool, hire a limousine. They may opt out of the market, in other words, setting in motion a process of *adverse selection.*

These different responses from robbers and nonrobbers to a change in the effective price of taxi services can lead to a situation where a higher ratio of robbers to nonrobbers arises in the population of young black men who actually elect to hail taxis, than would obtain if the drivers were stopping readily for them. In other words, two equilibria may exist in this little model of the taxicab market—one where drivers suppose that a group is not overly threatening and so stop readily, in which case everyone in the group is happy to take a taxi; and another where drivers suppose the group is threatening and are slow to stop, in which case nonrobbers selectively opt out from hailing taxis, confirming the drivers' fears.

Now, I have invented this hypothetical situation for illustrative purposes. I do not think it explains crime statistics on the streets in New York City, or that it provides a good empirical account of why robbery rates are higher among young black men than they are among older white women (if, as seems plausible to suppose, they are). It is a conceptual device meant to show how racial markings can come to have an informative role in people's decision making, and how the logic of self-interest on both sides—among drivers and their prospective customers—might reinforce the informational role of racial markings. In a statistically discriminatory equilibrium where racial markings are correlated with certain behaviors, those markings have informational value, and it is difficult to see how anyone could unilaterally withdraw from such a world. This way of thinking leaves scholars with a fairly robust account of the phenomenon at issue. When informed by the biologists that "there are no (biological—taxonomic) races," one still knows that there is information in a racial marker, and one's best response to that information may be to take an action that is contingent on race, thereby pushing the equilibrium along. People cannot unilaterally withdraw from social conventions of this sort.

I could tell this story over and over: "If a few of 'those people' move into our neighborhood, pretty soon the neighborhood will be all Black, after which it is not going to be such a nice place to live—property values will fall, and we will lose our equity in this modest home," a White resident might think. So when one of "them" moves in, the incumbents sell or look around to see who might be selling: Oh my God, the Smiths are selling, the Joneses are selling. We'd better get out before it's too late. It is easy to see how such thinking could give rise to a self-fulfilling prophecy.

My point here regarding the nature of race is a subtle one. Let people believe that fluctuations of the stock market can be predicted by changes in sunspot activity. This may be true because, as an objective meteorological matter, sunspots correlate with rainfall, which influences crop yields, thus affecting the economy. Or, solar radiation might somehow influence the human psyche by altering how people behave in securities markets. These are objective causal links between sunspots and stock prices. They can be likened to grounding one's cognizance of race on the validity of a race-based biological taxonomy. But suppose that no objective links of this kind between sunspots and stock prices exist. Still, if enough people believe in the connection, monitor conditions on the sun's surface, and act based on how they anticipate security prices will be affected, then a real link between these evidently disparate phenomena will have been forged out of the subjective perceptions of stock market participants. At that point, belief in the financial relevance of sunspot activity will have been rendered entirely rational.

Similarly, no objective racial taxonomy need be valid for the study of subjective use of racial classifications to become warranted. It is enough that influential social actors hold schemes of racial classification in their minds, and act on those schemes. Their methods of classification may be mutually inconsistent, one with another, and they may be unable to give a cogent justification for adopting their schemes. But once a person knows that others in society will classify him on the basis of certain markers, and should these acts of classification affect his material or psychological well-being, then it will be a rational cognitive stance—not a belief in magic and certainly not a moral error—for him to think of himself as being raced. In turn, the fact that he thinks of himself in this way and the fact that his societal peers are inclined to classify him similarly can provide a compelling reason for a newcomer to society to adopt this ongoing scheme of racial classification. Learning the extant "language" of embodied social signification is a first step toward assimilation of the foreigner, or the newborn, into any raced society. I conclude that races, in the social–cognitive sense, may come to exist and to be reproduced over generations in a society, even though there may exist no races in the biological–taxonomic sense.

But, can this cognitive use of racial categorization be morally justified? Just as one might think it wrong to punish "witches" for the crime of being the devil's servant when in point of fact no people actually are, so too one might think it wrong to condition one's dealings with others on the basis of race when, in point of fact, there are no biological–taxonomic races. If there are no races, then what possible justification can there be for the embrace of racial identity? My view is that the existence of races in the biological–taxonomic sense, and the ethics of the practice of racial classification are largely distinct problems. What is more, I do not think people can get at the latter problem by interrogating the human heart, one person at a time. It is a mistake, in my view, to judge the propriety of social conventions in terms of whether individuals behave virtuously or viciously when they elect to comply with those conventions. To be taken seriously, an ethical critique of race-based thinking must get beneath (or behind) the cognitive acts of individual persons and investigate the structure of social relations within which those individuals operate.

Why Is Racial Inequality so Stubbornly Persistent?

This brings me to the topic of racial stigma and the associated notion of biased social cognition. These are to my mind the central innovative concepts in my book. My basic approach to the problem of racial inequality is cognitive not normative. I eschew use of the word racism not to avoid sounding like an outdated civil rights leader, but because the word is imprecise. More useful, I think, is my concept of biased social cognition. To see what I am getting at here, consider the taxicab example discussed above. Suppose, in the context of this example, there are two racial groups that are identical *ex ante,* but turn out to have different robbery rates *ex post* because of the adverse selection process (where non-robbers opt out if their group is thought by drivers to be threatening, thereby confirming the drivers' suspicions). Now, how might the drivers explain to themselves this observed racial disparity? If the drivers understand this group difference in behavior as a reflection of the fact that the groups are objectively different in the distribution of some underlying trait that leads people to rob taxis, then I would say they adopt an essentialist account of the racial inequality. Alternatively, the drivers might adopt a more sophisticated account, recognizing that the observed group difference has been created through social interaction. They might think, in other words, that they are witnessing a racial disparity in the creation of which all taxi market participants are implicated.

These are two distinct accounts that the drivers (or any observer of this situation, for that matter) might settle upon. One is an account that sees the racial inequality as an expression of some deeper, intrinsic disparity between the groups. Its source is exogenous. It is not a collective product but merely reflects differences between the populations. The other is an account that sees the inequality as an endogenous product of social interaction—something of society's collective making that emerges in the equilibrium, with no group necessarily being at fault.

Now what if the second account—where racial inequality is an endogenous product of social interaction—is the true one, but an observer adopts the first account as an explanation for racial inequality? (That is, the observer concludes the groups are just different in some relevant respect, when in fact the groups are identical but, for reasons already explained, exhibit different equilibrium robbery rates conditional on hailing a taxi.) Arriving at and holding such a false causal attribution is what I call biased social cognition: The observer's cognitive processes of accounting for what he sees are biased in such a way that exogenous, group-based differences are seen as the source of a racial disparity, when its actual cause is endogenous and has little to do with group traits.

I wish to stress that racial stigma is not a bludgeon with which I hope to beat "whitey" into political submission. It does not refer to sinister thoughts in the heads of Whites. Nor is it an invitation to passivity for Blacks. Rather, what I am doing with this concept is trying to move from the fact that people take note of racial classification in the course of their interactions with one another, to some understanding of how this affects their perceptions of the phenomena they observe in the social world around them, and how it shapes their explanations of those phenomena. I am asking, When does the race of those subject to some problematic social circumstance affect whether powerful observers perceive a problem, and if so, what follows from this?

Given the evident sensitivity of racial discourses, it is perhaps best if I make the point with a nonracial example. So, consider gender inequality, disparity in the social outcomes for boys and girls, in two different venues—schools and jails. Suppose that, when compared to the girls, the boys are overrepresented among those doing well in math and science in the schools, and also among those doing poorly in society at large by ending up in jail. There is some evidence to support both suppositions, but only the first is widely perceived to be a problem for public policy. Why? I would answer that this disparity between boys and girls in the technical curriculum offends people's basic intuition about the propriety of underlying social processes. Although people may not be able to determine exactly why this outcome occurs, they instinctively know that it is not right. In the face of the disparity society is inclined to interrogate its institutions—to search the record of social practice and examine myriad possibilities in order to see where things might have gone wrong. Baseline expectation is that equality should prevail here. Moral sensibility is offended when it does not. And so, an impetus to reform is spurred. Society cannot easily envision a wholly legitimate sequence of events that would produce the disparity, so it attempts the task of solving a problem.

On the other hand, gender disparity in rates of imprisonment occasions no such disquiet. This is because, tacitly if not explicitly, people are "gender essentialists." That is, they think boys and girls are different in some ways relevant to explaining the disparity—different either in biological natures, or in deeply ingrained socializations. (Note well, the essentialism with which I am concerned need not be based solely or even mainly in biology. It can be grounded in possibly false beliefs about profound cultural difference as well.) The intuitions of gender essentialists are not offended by the fact of vastly higher rates of imprisonment among males than females. People seldom ask any deeper questions about why this disparity has come about. And so, they see no problem.

Now, society may be right or wrong to act as it does in these gender-disparity matters, but my point is to show with the example that the bare facts of gender disparity do not, in themselves, suggest any course of action. To act, one must marry the facts to some model of social causation. This model need not be explicit in one's mind. It can and usually will lurk beneath the surface of conscious reflections. Still, it is the facts plus the model that lead people to perceive a given circumstance as indicative or nonindicative of some as yet undiagnosed failing in social interactions. This kind of reflection on the deeper structure of social–cognitive processes, as they bear on issues of racial disparity, is what I had hoped to encourage with my discussion of biased social cognition. And, the role of race in such processes is what I am alluding to when I talk about racial stigma.

To show how the argument goes, I would like to invoke a thought experiment not unlike the ones I analyze at length in my book. Imagine that an observer correctly takes note of the fact that, on the average and all else equal, commercial loans to Blacks pose a greater risk of default, or that Black residential neighborhoods are more likely to decline. This may lead that observer to withhold credit from Blacks, or to move away from any neighborhood when more than a few Blacks move into it. But what if race conveys this information only because, when a great number of observers expect it to do so and act on that expectation, the result (through some possibly complex chain of social causation) is to bring about the confirmation of their beliefs? Perhaps Blacks default more often precisely because they have trouble getting further extensions of credit in the face of a crisis. Or, perhaps non-Black residents panic at the arrival of a few Blacks, selling their homes too quickly and below the market value to lower-income Black buyers, and it is this process that ends up promoting neighborhood decline.

If under such circumstances observers were to attribute racially disparate behaviors to deeply ingrained biological or cultural limitations of Blacks—thinking, perhaps, that Blacks do not repay their loans or take care of their property because, for whatever reasons, they are just less responsible people on average—then these observers might well be mistaken. Yet since their surmise about Blacks is supported by hard evidence, they might well persist in the error. Such an error, if persistent, would be of great political moment, because if one attributes an endogenous difference (a difference produced within a system of interactions) to an exogenous cause (a cause located outside that system), then one is unlikely to see any need for systemic reform. This distinction between endogenous and exogenous sources of social causation, I am arguing, is the key to understanding the difference in reformist intuitions about gender inequalities in schools and in jails: because people think the disparity of school outcomes stems from endogenous sources, while the disparity of jail outcomes is tacitly attributed in most causal models to exogenous sources, they are differentially moved to do something about the disparities.

So, the effect I seek when I talk about racial stigma, and the reason I employ an apparently loaded phrase like biased social cognition, is this: It is a politically consequential cognitive distortion to understand the observably disadvantageous position of a racially defined population subgroup as having emerged from qualities taken to be intrinsic to the group when, as a matter of actual social causation, that disadvantage is the product of a system of social interactions. I stress that it hardly matters whether those internal qualities mistakenly seen as the source of a group's observed laggardly status are biological or deeply cultural. What matters, I argue, is that something has gone wrong if observers fail to see systemic, endogenous interactions that lead to negative social outcomes for Blacks, and instead attribute those results to exogenous factors taken as internal to the group in question. My contention is that in American society, when the group in question is Blacks, the risk of this kind of causal misattribution is especially great.

I believe the disparate impact of the enforcement of antidrug laws and antiprostitution offers a telling illustration of the value in this way of thinking. There can be no drug market without sellers and buyers, and no street prostitution without hookers and johns. Typically, those on the selling side of such markets are more deeply involved in crime and disproportionately drawn from the bottom rungs of society. When society entertains alternative responses to the social malady reflected in drug use or in street prostitution, it must weight the costs likely to be imposed upon the people involved. Tacit models of social causation will play a role in this process of evaluation. To ruin a college student's life because of a drug buy, or a businessman's reputation because of a pickup in the red-light district, may seem far more costly than to send a young "thug" to Riker's Island, or to put a "floozy" behind bars. One consequence of racial stigma, I suggest, is that because those bearing the brunt of the cost of the punitive response to the broad social malady of drug usage are disproportionately black, society is less impelled to examine what it is undertaking in this area of policy, and to consider reform. How serious a given crime is seen to be in the minds of those who through their votes indirectly determine our policies, and how deserved the punishment for a given infraction, can depend on the racial identities of the parties involved. This, I am holding, is human nature. There need be nothing sinister in any of it. But, if people want to analyze what is going on around them, and not merely to moralize about it, they will want to take such possibilities seriously.

That is what I see myself as doing. I use the theory of biased social cognition that I have just sketched to argue that durable racial inequality can best be understood as the outgrowth of a series of "vicious circles of cumulative causation." Tacit association of "Blackness" with "unworthiness" in the American public's imagination affects cognitive processes and promotes essentialist causal misattributions. Confronted by facts of racially disparate achievement, racially disproportionate transgression of legal strictures, and racially unequal development of productive potential, observers will have difficulty identifying with the plight of a group of people whom they mistakenly think are simply reaping what they have sown. So, there will be little public support for egalitarian policies benefiting a stigmatized racial group. This, in turn, encourages the reproduction through time of racial inequality because, absent some policies of this sort, the low social conditions of many Blacks persist, the negative social meanings ascribed to Blackness are thereby reinforced, and so the racially biased social–cognitive processes are reproduced, completing the circle.

What Is Racial Justice?

What is more, I argue in *The Anatomy of Racial Inequality* that this situation constitutes a gross historical injustice in American society. Present racial inequality is a justice problem because it has its root in past unjust acts that were perpetrated on the basis of race. Because of past racial injustice indifference to present racial inequality cannot be tolerated. To see why this matters, suppose it could be shown that a posture of official public indifference to racial inequality would enhance comity and community. (So, it would seem, many advocates of a "color-blind" America believe.) Even so, I would still want to urge that some efforts to reduce racial inequality would be warranted. However, I do not think that the degree to which social policy should be oriented toward reducing present racial inequality—the weight to be placed on this objective in the social-decision calculus, if you will—can or should be conceived in terms of correcting or balancing for historical violation. This is what leads me to reject a broad-scale program of slavery reparations. In my view, although the quantitative attribution of causal weight to distant historical events required by reparations advocacy is not workable, one can still support qualitative claims.

Advocates of slavery reparations conceive the problem of morally problematic racial history in compensatory terms. By contrast, I propose to see the problem in interpretative terms. That is, I seek public recognition of the severity, and the crucial contemporary relevance, of what has transpired. The goal is to encourage a common basis of historical memory—a common narrative—through which past racial injury and its continuing significance can enter into current policy discourse. What is required for racial justice, as I conceive it, is a commitment on the part of the public, the political elite, and the opinion-shaping media to take responsibility for the plight of the urban Black poor, and to understand this troubling circumstance in a general way as having emerged out of an ethically indefensible past. Such a commitment should, in my view, be open-ended and not contingent on demonstrating any specific lines of causality.

I also take the strong position in the book that the goal of *race blindness*—which many take to be the touchstone of public morality in matters of race—is, in fact, a false ideal. This is the final point I wish to make, exploring the question of in what does racial justice consist. I will be direct. The United States has a morally problematic history around questions of race. I am talking here about slavery, lynching, Jim Crow segregation. And significant racial inequality currently exists. What is the relevance of this history to moral assessment of the current situation? Some people say that the issue is one of rights—the significance of this history is to show how badly things go awry when people's rights are not respected. These people generally argue that over the last half-century U.S. society has made steady progress in establishing a regime where individual rights are respected—from *Brown v. Topeka Board of Education* onward—and that the country veers from this reform path to the extent that it engages in so-called "reverse discrimination." In other words, they argue "two wrongs don't make a right." They stress that society needs to fairly establish rules mandating equal treatment regardless of race. Society had them wrong for a long time, but the point is to get the rules right. The problem with affirmative action, these people say, is that it violates the rules in the interest of trying to do the right thing. But since the original problem was one of rule violation, these people argue that reliance on affirmative action is a big mistake.

Another group of people argue that America's morally problematic history created a debt, that America owes Black people payment for the wrongs done, for unrequited labor during slavery and less than equal citizenship during the century following the end of slavery. "Here's the bill, I want to get paid," they say in effect. For these people, the issue is not a matter of rights—at least, not rights to the "equal protection of the laws." Rather, they make a tort argument based upon the presumption that just recompense is due. I disagree with both of those groups of people, with both of those arguments. Let me try to say why.

I do not think that racial inequality is any longer mainly a rights problem. This view, which is arguable, is based both upon empirical judgment as well as on my more theoretical arguments. While there is not space here to review the literature that supports this claim, in my opinion it has become impossible to account for racial disparity in American society by reference to overt acts of racial discrimination. I am not saying there is no discrimination, for we know from a variety of sources that there is plenty of it. What I am saying is that the amount of racial inequality accounted for by such continuing discrimination is proportionately less today than was the case 20 years ago; less now than 40 years ago; and very much less now than was the case 60 years ago. Increasingly, racial group disparity in economic standing in American society rests upon average racial differences in acquired capacities to function in a modern economy. (I'm talking here mainly about the situation of Blacks, but the observation could be extended.) Now, I hasten to add that I do not attribute this disparity to genes.

My model is one in which disparate outcomes such as that are seen as products of interactive social processes. In my view, human beings develop not as disembodied machines in which a certain amount of human capital has or has not been invested, but as situated persons tied up with other persons in networks of mutual social intercourse through which flow all manner of resources that facilitate human development—starting with the family and moving out from there. This difference in capacities to function, a difference in my view increasingly implicated in racial inequality, is not a manifestation of something intrinsically different about the groups. It is a social product, it is endogenous, and it is something for which I want to say everyone has a responsibility, in which everyone plays a role.

Viewed in this way, the racial inequality problem is not mainly due to a failure to extend equal rights to all citizens. I argue in my book that if people think racial disparity is a problem and people want to do something about it, then they have to regard the inequality in and of itself as morally troubling. One ought not, in other words, to limit moral scrutiny to the procedures governing transactions among persons, but should extend critical gaze to the substantive social relations that obtain between people belonging to different racial groups and that help to reproduce racial differences in acquired capacities across the generations. Again, I do not mean to be obscure or abstract or talk in euphemism. What I am saying here is that ghettos—residential segregation or nonrandom geographic distribution of populations by income and race that produces a clustering of poor minority group members—will result in varied opportunities for human development across segregated residential communities. Some communities will be felicitous of human flourishing and development, and others will be destructive of it; and poor minority group members will be disproportionately concentrated in communities of the latter kind.

Now, such a situation need not present a problem of rights. It will be a problem of rights around the margins. To the extent that realtors are discriminating, that landlords are discriminating, that restrictive covenants are in effect, that banks practice redlining—to that extent occurs a problem of rights. But as Tom Schelling, my friend and mentor and a great economist, taught a long time ago, one does not need to have individuals acting on motives of invidious racial antagonism in order to get pronounced differences in geographic location. Schelling's famous tipping model (1978) will work even if only a few people around the margin are mildly concerned about the racial composition or the kind of community that they live in. Then, as they move out and the community's racial composition changes, a few more people in that neighborhood are pushed to the margin and decide to move out too. The cumulative effect of such a process can be stark residential segregation by race, even though most individuals have only a mild preference for living near their own kind.

Schelling (1978) illustrates his idea by inviting us to imagine an extended checkerboard with alternating light and dark squares, as one randomly places red and black checkers. Then, adopt the rule that a checker stays put unless it happens to be a minority in its neighborhood. (On a checkerboard, any square has a "neighborhood" of eight other squares around it. So there are nine in any neighborhood.) If a red checker finds four or fewer red checkers in its nine-square neighborhood, it moves. This is a very mild preference for own-association. Yet the only stable configuration under this relocation rule is complete segregation because, with nine squares in a fully occupied neighborhood, some group is necessarily going to be in the minority, and thus on the move.

This little example illustrates an important point: aggregate patterns of geographic location exhibiting stark racial separation can be the product of microlevel decisions in which the desire for own-race association is very mild. Now if developmental opportunity goes alongside residential location, then that result may be stark racial disparity of such opportunity. If history has left one group of people relatively less well endowed with developmental resources, then patterns of residential segregation by race lead to disparate developmental opportunities by race that, in turn, imply that racial inequality will be perpetuated. But, if this racial inequality is ultimately due to a problematic past, then its possibly indefinite perpetuation via interactive processes that do not in themselves violate anybody's rights nevertheless constitutes a serious social injustice.

This, for me, is the fundamental moral question when people talk about racial justice: Do we want to do something about inequality or not? This is why I stress the difference between blindness and neutrality—or, equivalently, the distinction between rules of conduct (people must not discriminate on the basis of race) and the goals of public action (people need to move toward a world where there is less racial inequality). I am elevating the latter, goal-oriented moral conception over the former, process-oriented one. The latter is a defensible moral imperative for the United States. The next question becomes how to get there. But I want to get the order of questions correct. Deciding on a goal is the first order of business; electing the methods for moving toward the goal is a secondary consideration. I wish not to enshrine colorblindness (the idea that people simply must not take any cognizance of others' race) as the racial-justice ideal and leave it at that. That is a recipe for racial inequality to remain stubbornly persistent.

Let me stress that this is not just about an advocacy for affirmative action policies. My position is that affirmative action policies ought not be ruled out as a matter of high principle—the idea that color blindness is the embodiment of our commitment to racial fairness. Instead, I would want affirmative action policies to be employed in situations when it would be prudent to do so, taking full account of all ramifications arising from making use of this particular policy instrument. Sometimes its use is plausible, prudent, not especially disruptive or costly, and sometimes not.

Thus, I wish that there were fewer young Black men in prison today, but I would not advise affirmative action in the criminal justice system as a response to that condition. "You do the crime, you do the time," ought to apply equally to all criminal defendants regardless of race. Now, one can debate how much time should be done for this or that crime. But I would want those rules applied without taking note of the race of people subject to them. However, I hold this view not because I believe that in the abstract and in every situation ignoring race is the primary moral imperative. Rather, I hold this view because in a courtroom, impartial procedure is the most important outcome of the enterprise. A courtroom produces a judgment concerning whether the person accused is guilty and, if so, what punishment is indicated. But, the courtroom also produces the process through which that judgment is arrived at, and the principal public desire is that this process be impartial. It is this impartiality that legitimates the court's authority in the eyes of the public. And therefore, to reject affirmative action in the courtroom, despite an abiding concern about racial inequality in the burden of criminal punishment, is not an implication of some high principle of race blindness. Instead, this position follows from the special nature of that particular proceeding—where blindness of process is the most important outcome being produced. And I note that admitting a freshman class to a state university is not such an enterprise. I am here making a distinction between the public act of judging a defendant's guilt or innocence (where impartiality is absolutely central), and the public act of admitting a freshman class (where all manner of compromise and consideration go into the final determination about who should be included).

I wish not to make color blindness into a totem. The headline of my argument is that color blindness, as a rule of public conduct, is not closed to moral deviation. A system of rules is closed to moral deviation if it is always possible to correct the consequences of rule violation by actions that are themselves in conformity with the rules. That is a plausible condition for any set of rules that are to be applied systematically, since rules will sometimes be violated and one will want to respond to the conditions of that violation. And if one cannot do so without further violating the rule, then the very idea of this system of rules as a guide to moral action is problematic. I argue in my book that color blindness is like this. It is a system of rules that has not always been respected, and the consequences of this historic violation cannot be effectively reversed without taking race into account in some way or another. So for me the questions then become when, how, where, and for what reasons will race be taken into account. I reject the high-minded opting out of the race game altogether by those who say, "Oh, those were all wrongful actions in the past, and we are simply not going to do that anymore."

SUMMARY AND CONCLUSION

I will close by returning to the issue of slavery reparations, and to the subject of my Christian faith. My deepest reasons for being leery of reparations are religious. The reparations argument is a transactional, not a relational one. It is a we–they argument, seeking a quid pro quo. "They did this to us, and we are owed." It permits the following: The day after the payments are made, should they be made, non-Black Americans can disengage and go on about their business because their obligation has been discharged with the reparations payment.

Imagine a man walking in front of your house who slips and breaks a leg. His lawyer calls your lawyer. A settlement is agreed, and you do not expect to see him anymore. He has been paid. I hold that the obligations of mutuality entailed by the conflicted racial history of the United States are not such things as that. They cannot and ought not to be dischargeable in such a way. They are not fungible; this is not something that ought to be for sale. One cannot escape racial conundrums that easily. I can put this point in another way: America has unfinished business from the post-Civil War reconstruction, from the Fourteenth and Fifteenth Amendments. When I go to the south side of Chicago, or to east Detroit or to north Philadelphia, or south central Los Angeles, I see unfinished business. I also see in these places a sacred, civic obligation calling society to address the unfinished business. By "sacred, civic obligation" I mean that this is a matter that goes right to the heart of American identity: it is about the national soul. The richest, most powerful country on earth, the heart of its great cities, contains the most desperate, horrific places to live that can be found anywhere in the industrial West. One can travel for years in northern Europe and never see anything like what one can see driving for 15 minutes in most big American cities. This is not an easy problem, I know, and I am not wagging my finger to complain that Americans have, for lack of moral will, yet to make it all go away. (Remember, my argument is that complex social processes implicating all of society lie at the heart of this problem.) Nevertheless, it is unfinished business; it is a blot on American civilization. It should not be. And, this is a "sacred, civic" matter.

I am aware of the church-state problems here. I am not referring to any religious tradition when using the term sacred. I mean to suggest, however, that it is a matter that goes right to the core of who Americans are as a people. And, nothing about it ought to be for sale. I see something profane about the idea that this civic obligation to rectify the consequences of past rule-violation can be cashed out. America ought not to be dealing with this problem in that way—separate camps of citizens negotiating with one another from either side of a conference table about how much is to be handed over. Society ought to be committed to working together to resolve these problems. (I realize I have not laid out a program of action in my book, but one cannot do everything in 200 pages.) Americans ought to be committed to working together on this problem for as long as it takes until the problem is solved. I tell Black audiences exactly the same things I am writing here.

Finally, I wish to note that, amidst all of this argument and advocacy, I have not lost sight of higher ground. I have not forgotten what the apostle Peter says in Acts 10. You may recall that in this scriptural passage Peter is uncertain whether the gospel has been sent only for the Jews, or is intended for Gentiles as well. He has a dream. An angel comes with a blanket filled with animals. The angel beckons Peter to kill and eat, whence Peter objects that according to Jewish law such animals are unclean. The angel says to Peter, in effect, who are you to turn away as unclean that which God has cleansed? And then, suddenly, the scales fall from Peter's eyes. He then grasps the true message in the dream, which is that "God is no respecter of persons but in every nation, he that feareth Him and worketh righteousness is accepted with Him." His mandate becomes to take the gospel first to a Roman centurion, Cornelius, and Cornelius' family, but then beyond.

"God is no respecter of persons." My theology-student friends tell me that in Greek the word person invokes connotations of "persona," "mask," "visage," "front." God does not care about one's looks. If people fear him and are righteous, then no matter what their "nation" he will accept them. God cares about what is in the heart. So the biologists, anthropologists, and population geneticists have had their say about the genetic unity of the human family, but here is a rather different argument. All are one people because they are creatures made in the image of God. I have not lost sight of that fact. I do not want us divided into camps.

The challenge to Christian scholars of every stripe is to provide advocacy to the disenfranchised and downtrodden by using academic training to promote rigor in the study of important social issues that plague society. And at the same time, Christian scholars should take advantage of their unique Christian perspective that recognizes that all people are spiritual creatures, first and foremost. Only then can one fully capture the human experience and fulfill the spiritual obligation as stated in the second great commandment: to love our neighbors as we love ourselves (Matt 22:39).

Chapter 5

A Philosophy of Economics

Michael Novak

INTRODUCTION

My philosophy of economics emerges, not from formal training in economics, but from my own particular experiences. I do not claim this to be a definitive "philosophy of economics," only an expression of my intellectual journey from sympathy for collectivist control of the economy to embracing market capitalism fully as the most effective way to organize contemporary economies.

Let me begin this way: Business is a noble Christian vocation, a work of social justice, and the single greatest institutional hope of the poor of the world, if the poor are to move up out of poverty (Novak, *Business as a Calling* 1996; 2002). Only business, especially small business, creates new, independent, and progress-generating jobs.

In Latin America, Africa, the Middle East, and Asia—to the one side—are an immense number of poor people either underemployed or unemployed. To the other side is an immense amount of work to be done. There are homes, clinics, and schools to be built; sanitation to be supplied to villages and cities; and lights, refrigerators, and simple ovens to be manufactured for those who lack them, so that their children can live decently. All that work is to be done; and

The author would like to thank Grattan T. Brown for outstanding work in executing the footnotes, under the author's direction.

all those good people are looking for work. Who will bring these two together, like two live wires now held apart? Who will bring these two wires together to generate the spark of development? That is the role of entrepreneurs: to match people seeking work with all the work desperately needing to be done. The vocation of business is the single most strategic vocation in the work of social justice. It is the vocation most necessary for lifting the poor out of poverty. Business creates jobs where jobs did not exist before.

Yet as a recent issue of the *Religious Studies Review* demonstrates (Reiger, 2002), many scholars in this nation's divinity schools voice disdain for business corporations and even for the business vocation. All that remains on the Left, after the fall of real existing socialism, is anticapitalism. Anticapitalism is the single broad cause that has for generations united both the Leninist and social democratic Left *with* the traditionalist Right. From the Right and the Left, there are century-old arguments against capitalism, business, and (the current buzzword) neoliberalism (for example, Bourdieu, 1998). The collapse of socialism did not make this hostility to capitalism go away. This hostility is older and deeper than socialism. This hostility is not hard to understand, and I once shared it myself. Poets, romantics, and mystics have been hostile to any and all economic systems that have ever existed—socialist, feudal, mercantile, traditionalist, and all those current economic regimes of the Third World. But the hostility toward capitalism has a particularly broad "spiritual" or quasi-religious passion behind it. Capitalism is rejected, not as less practical or less effective than other systems, but as in some way corrupting, immoral, even *evil.*

The source of this hostility, I believe, lies in a profound philosophical error. On the Left, that source is not empirical. Even when any factual argument is rebutted—even when it is conceded that capitalism *is* in fact more productive, efficient, and economically creative—still, it will be argued that capitalism is immoral. This judgment seems to flow from a certain habit of wishfulness, dreaminess, or perhaps more accurate, utopianism, in the light of which the humble, vulgar realism of capitalism appears to be an outrageous surrender to the unworthy. On the Right, the source of hostility to capitalism appears to be nostalgia for the high courtesy, chivalry, and noblesse oblige of the aristocratic, land-based order of the precapitalist, preliberal world. Both Left and Right compare capitalism not to any historical system that has actually existed, but to an ideal of perfection as they imagine it. A more just and realistic assumption would be this: just as one should not expect too much from democracy, so one should not expect too much from capitalism. Both are flawed systems, just as human beings themselves are flawed.

Perhaps I am wrong in this diagnosis of the sources of hostility to capitalism. If I am, the larger point stands forth all the more starkly: Simply in order to *understand* the vocation of business in the highly ideological world of the American university today, a young woman or man about to make crucial life-choices needs to engage in a decent amount of philosophic inquiry.

In fact, there are at least three levels of discourse in which a philosophy of economics is both necessary and useful, both for those about to choose a career and for those already engaged in business, who need from time to time to explain themselves to their critics. Indeed, a clearly held philosophy of economic life ought to be of benefit both to veterans and to new entrants in the field, because of the light it sheds on the treacherous terrain economists all need to traverse. Here I can provide no more than a sketch. I hope that putting part of it in autobiographical terms may help younger people, especially, to follow along with me. I begin with the first level of inquiry.

THE FIRST LEVEL: TO ADJUDICATE AMONG ECONOMIC IDEOLOGIES

At some point at the end of my graduate studies, I decided that I needed to turn my philosophical and theological interests toward the study of economics. By training, I was accustomed to thinking in an anticapitalist vein, just as one trained in the humanities learns to abjure "bourgeois" tastes, and to admire the aristocratic manner. Who as a young humanist did not want to belong to "the aristocracy of the spirit"? To be described as a "prince of a man" put a glow in the heart. What young woman failed to know that, if people could but see it, she was a "princess"?

But, think about this. How odd it is that humanists disdain "bourgeois" tendencies and "philistine" habits, when in fact nearly all the beautiful lace, millinery, tapestries, and clothing, and nearly all the most elegant wines, best cheeses, and most beautifully wrought swords, cutlery, and woodwork of the West have been executed by the bourgeoisie. The bourgeoisie are precisely those who are neither lords nor serfs, but skilled craftsmen living independently by their wits. In contrast, real princes and princesses in centuries past seemed to spend an undue amount of time murdering their own relatives, or sending them to the Tower. Few aristocrats produced even a single beautiful object of art.

In other words, the humanities teach an aristocratic ideology rather sharply at variance with the real world. The aristocratic ideology carries with it a profound contempt for business, businessmen, and a capitalist way of life. It is rooted in a premodern vision of life, is radically opposed to modernity, and conveys the bitter taste of *resentment.* The rise of the businessman has typically been accompanied by a decline in the wealth, status, and self-importance of princes, dukes, counts, lords, and barons.

From the Left, I was instructed by Paul Tillich at Harvard (and not by him alone), that a Christian theologian *must* be a socialist. It went without saying that capitalism was not aristocratic but vulgar and ethically corrupt. None that I encountered supposed, even as a hypothesis, that capitalism could be a *moral* system. Its immorality or amorality was simply a given.

As a young man, I was fairly easily persuaded by the aristocrats and the socialists. My own family was quite poor, and in Johnstown, Pennsylvania, the mill owners lived on the hill up above the workers. On the other hand, a question nagged at me. I could not help remembering that a part of my family had not immigrated to America when all four of my grandparents came, separately, from the mountain regions of Slovakia in Central Europe around 1900. Our European relatives were living under Soviet socialism—not under that tepid "Christian socialism" of which Marx and Engels wrote with disgust. Later writers liked to call the Soviet Union "real existing socialism" (1848, ch. 3). The rolling Soviet tanks that had crushed the Prague Spring of 1968 were a vivid reminder to me of what my European relatives lived under.

Therefore, I had mixed feelings about socialism—and also about capitalism. I was strongly pulled toward socialism, but something warned me to hold back. And that is why I began my study of economics. Both of necessity and by choice, my study would be that of the philosopher and theologian, not that of the graduate student who wished to become a professional economist, nor that of the student in a School of Business or Management. I wanted to reach a point of view that would allow me, on some valid independent grounds, to reach a decision between rival ideologies.

Is it more reasonable, I was asking myself, to commit to a career of promoting a mild form of socialism and denigrating capitalism? Or to a career, unlikely as it then seemed to me, of taking a stand *against* socialism? It is important to note that these alternatives, as I saw them, were asymmetrical: I could oppose socialism without really embracing capitalism. Many academics did that in those days, and even today. I could also embrace socialism, and *along* with it, its explicit and intense opposition to capitalism. At that time, I could hardly imagine actually praising capitalism from a moral point of view.

I need to mention that along with the great sociologist Peter Berger and some others, I twice spent two weeks or so in Cuernavaca, Mexico, teaching in Father Ivan Illich's Institute. My subject in one of those years was something like "The Theology of Revolution." The problem of the poor of Latin America and elsewhere worried me, but my point of view was political rather than economic. Even then I could feel in every strain of my argument the need for greater economic knowledge. In fact, I was deeply impressed that my colleague, Peter Berger, for whom I had much admiration, was just then talking about his own research in economics.

Berger had been making a sociological study of economic development. Although he had begun with a socialist paradigm in mind, he had become fascinated by the surprising empirical picture emerging from economic statistics in South Korea, Taiwan, Singapore, and Hong Kong. It was from him, I believe, that I first heard the term "the Four Asian Tigers." He had begun a book, *Pyramids of Sacrifice* (1974), in which he was arguing that both capitalist and socialist systems seemed to be abandoning huge swaths of people to unnecessary and uncalled-for poverty: "A plague on both your houses!" Later, sustained exposure to East Asia made him begin to reconsider. He encountered unassailable evidence that capitalism had the capacity to transform economies from extreme poverty to rather stunning development, even in the short time of twenty or so years.

From Aristotle, I had learned in my first year of studying philosophy a deep respect for collecting specimens, whether of botanical, biological, political, or ethical forms of life, before attempting to make evaluative judgments. That seemed to me the right way to proceed in trying to adjudicate the question between ideological points of view. To begin with, it was clear to me that socialists explicitly proposed an ideology, because when they began they had not a single existing example to point to. By contrast, liberals (those in favor of free markets) claimed to be practical, not ideological, arguing from the success of existing practice.

In reply, socialists countered that, even though capitalists may not think they have an ideology, capitalists act from a false consciousness and according to their own interests—both out of kilter with reality. In fact, they said, capitalism is doomed to self-destruction and will soon be swept into the dustbin of history. Inexorably the world is moving toward collectivization, they said; and the most rational and scientific organization of that world collective will be socialist. They called their viewpoint "scientific socialism," and it pulled like a magnetic North Star on the minds of many of the most influential social thinkers and intellectuals of Europe and America. Even those who were not complete Marxists adopted an anticapitalist tendency, along with an economic outlook that went as far as their own pragmatism would allow in measuring progress from the socialist point of view: "More active state: good! Free private enterprise: corrupt!" Communists spoke glowingly of the "progressive forces" of the world, in which they included those who adopted more or less pinkish shades of the Marxist worldview: anticapitalist, antibourgeois; a division of the world into the oppressors and the oppressed. That was about where I was in those days.

Beginning to Fashion a Philosophical Point of View

But I also knew I needed to step back a little, to gain a deeper point of view. Looking back, I can see now how much I relied upon scholars with far larger sets of empirical tools than I possessed for discovering what concepts, criteria, and methods to apply. I found most useful those scholars who had some serious commitment to socialist views themselves, for they had a knack of taking socialist claims seriously enough to reformulate them as empirical hypotheses. Although Sidney Hook's main interest (1974) lay in the area of political and civil freedoms rather than in economics, he was one of the first of the major American philosophers to move away from Marxism with clear practical reasons and a profound tragic sense. To a lesser but still useful extent, Irving Howe (1979, p. xiv) and other writers in *Dissent* helped too, if only by spelling out their own version of socialism, famously described in its first number as "the name of our dreams." In Britain, Stuart Hampshire and Leszek Kolokowski (1974) edited a splendid volume of essays in which a variety of socialists addressed the question: "What Went Wrong?" That is, why was not socialism anywhere working out as described in its theories? Michael Harrington in his earnestness and American love for concrete cases also provided much that was empirically testable (1968, particularly chap. 2). I learned to admire the intelligence and, in a large sense, fairness of Robert Heilbroner (1974, 1980). He could be quite polemical, but he was willing to admit mistakes.

But without question, the single best aid was the sustained work of Peter Berger over many years. First was the set of two books he edited on empirical studies of equality around the world (1987). Then, most conveniently of all, I absorbed his masterly summary book, *The Capitalist Revolution,* (1986) in which he formulated fifty empirically testable propositions typically advanced to demonstrate the superiority of socialism over capitalism. He went on to supply the evidence then available for assessing these propositions.

This is far from a complete inventory of the studies I eagerly sought out. F. A. Hayek's and Ludwig von Mises's books on socialism (Hayek, 1971, 1972; Mises, 1981) opened my eyes to the epistemological deficits of socialism. Without a price system, national commissars were simply blind to the strength and frequency of choices and desires. They were wholly without crucial information and therefore limited to guesswork. Igor Shafarevich (1980, esp. chap. "Socialism and Individuality") taught me the sources of the socialist passion for equality and uniformity: its dread of choice and difference.

Socialism, I concluded in *The Spirit of Democratic Capitalism* (1982), grows out of a great number of philosophical assumptions and radically erroneous ways of imagining the world, which go far beyond its mistaken economic theories. This is why many on the Left, after the humiliating collapse of socialism in 1989–1991, did not give up being leftists. The chairman of the Socialist Party of Chile told me, after asking for permission to publish *The Spirit of Democratic Capitalism* in Spanish under the Socialist Party imprint, "I would like to demonstrate to Chileans that socialism is not exhausted by the mistaken economic theories of the nineteenth century." In his hands in Chile, and in many other places, socialism mutated into a theory of culture and politics. It became a radical revolt against the Jewish and Christian view of the human body and human sexuality; it rebelled against Western culture's hard-won realism, prudence, and sense of limits. The Left is not bounded by economics: it has an appetite for the unlimited, the utopian, the dream.

In ethics today, therefore, the style of the Left is undisciplined by economics. It prefers rebellion, relativism, nihilism. The Left today expresses itself in massive protests such as those of the antiglobalization protestors in Seattle, Genoa, and Johannesburg, whose style always includes angry lawlessness. Its preferred philosophy today is postmodernism, a radical reduction of human reason to questions of power and interest. This deconstruction issues in nihilism, whose lightly disguised implication is that only the will-to-power matters. (The origins of Paul de Mans' postmodernism, not surprisingly, have the same roots as Nazism and Stalinism.) Mussolini defined totalitarianism quite simply as *"La feroce volontà!"*

All these post-1989 developments show that it would have been a grave mistake to understand socialism as merely a theory about economics. That was only a fraction of its appeal. One must approach questions about capitalism and socialism on a plane deeper than economics. One must take care to attend both to cultural and to political dimensions usually beyond the ken of economics.

Capitalism and Socialism not Symmetrical

On this plane, it turns out that capitalism and socialism are not symmetrical systems. One can speak abstractly of capitalism in more or less purely economic terms, with relatively little reference to questions of culture and politics, and still make limited sense. I do not believe that capitalism can be wholly captured or explained in this way; hence my own tripartite schema for talking about the three parts of the free society: economic, political, and moral-cultural. Still, the thriving libertarian movement shows that mine is not the only alternative (Murray, 1997; Boaz, 1997; Opitz, 1999).

By contrast, socialism is a far more sweeping and unitary system than capitalism. Politics and culture are as much a part of its essence, under its single collective system of control, as economics. Not for nothing is the primordial socialist flag one single color, red, without division. Under socialism, all things are pulled into one. It constitutes a religion, an ethic, a cultural force all its own. It has its own distinctive mystique, scorning the self-imposed limits of classic Western politics. Socialist man is and intends to be a *new man.* To understand socialism adequately, scholars have been forced to turn to philosophy and theology, beyond mere economics (Kolakowski, 1978).

By the same measure, economics alone turns out to be inadequate for understanding the success of capitalist economics, although for quite different reasons. Just twenty years ago (prior to 1989), on most of the broad surface of this planet, capitalist acts between consenting adults were treated as crimes against the state, punishable by death. Business corporations operated solely at the sufferance of the state, with no right to exist independently on their own. In this respect, too many economists and businessmen in the United States forgot in those days how much they depend upon a political regime of a certain type, respectful of rights of association, private property, and personal economic initiative. One can make sense of a capitalist economy in its own terms, with relatively little intermixture of political control or interference. Nonetheless, a capitalist economy is a fairly rare growth in world history. Few are the regimes that have allowed it the liberty to thrive; even fewer have nourished the specific cultural habits required for its flourishing. Until very recent centuries, there were none. Even where its fragile life seems to flourish, significant parties and interests within the state work relentlessly to submerge under political domination a free and creative capitalist economy.

More than that, large governmental systems and welfare agencies in modern states suffuse the thoughts, desires, and habits of entire peoples. Two debilitating features of democracy thus come into view. As Tocqueville (1969) predicted a century and a half ago, there is drift downward toward materialism and mediocrity—

on the one hand—combined with the taste for surrendering liberty to the paternal state, in exchange for reduced uncertainty, in the name of equality:

> I am trying to imagine under what novel features despotism may appear in the world. In the first place, I see an innumerable multitude of men, alike and equal, constantly circling around in pursuit of the petty and banal pleasures with which they glut their souls. Over this kind of men stands an immense, protective power, which is alone responsible for securing their enjoyment and watching over their fate. That power is absolute, thoughtful of detail, orderly, provident, and gentle. It would resemble parental authority if, father-like, it tried to prepare its charges for a man's life, but on the contrary, it only tries to keep them in perpetual childhood. (pp. 691–92)

Further, the social democratic state better rewards the middle class custodians of welfare benefits than it does the unemployed and the very poor, whom it thrusts into psychological dependency, helplessness, and resentment. In a word, political regimes culturally affect economic systems.

In addition, the culture and moral habits of people also condition their economic behavior. That is why a capitalist economy fares far better in some cultures than others.[1] It heavily depends on work habits, family patterns, and metaphysical or religious energies of particular sorts. It will time and again fail to function in cultures that lack the necessary cultural habits. The range of political and cultural systems within which capitalist systems can grow and thrive is fairly narrow. Certain cultural and political preconditions must be met, or else the whole system seems to go awry. Culture and politics are prior to economics, and supply necessary preconditions for it.

For the philosopher and the theologian, to sort out the chief political, economic, and cultural prerequisites of capitalist and socialist systems is a fairly daunting task. But it is also a richly rewarding one, of considerable use to economists, to the extent that it throws new light from new perspectives upon perplexities they face everyday, especially those involved with questions of development in a global framework. A developed philosophy of economic life, moreover, illuminates the political, cultural, and economic terrain for practical men and women, who must try to determine which economic system, and in which form, they wish to support. To identify and to promote those economic systems best suited to human flourishing (I am not supposing that there is only one), one needs all the philosophic and critical help one can get.

[1]Lawrence Harrison writes in *Culture Matters: How Values Shape Human Progress*:
Skepticism about the link between cultural values and human progress is found particularly in two disciplines: economics and anthropology. For many economists, it is axiomatic that appropriate economic policy effectively implemented will produce the same results without reference to culture. The problem here is the case of multicultural countries in which some ethnic groups do better than others, although all operate with the same economic signals. Examples are the Chinese minorities in Thailand, Malaysia, Indonesia, the Philippines, and the United States; the Japanese minorities in Brazil and the United States; the Basques in Spain and Latin America; and the Jews wherever they have migrated. (p. xxiv).

THE SECOND LEVEL: SORTING OUT THE NECESSARY CONCEPTS

In *The Spirit of Democratic Capitalism* (1982), I set forth three different disciplines of the new *theology* of economics for whose development I was calling. The same three are relevant for the new *philosophy* of economics, which in some ways is more urgent. The first level of discourse in a new philosophy of economics is the one in which I have so far been engaged, the comparison of alternative systems of economic organization (such as socialism and capitalism). As I have shown, that set of inquiries soon involves one in prior and more basic explorations, having to do with economic and human questions that must be faced in any and all systems of economic life. That is the second level of discourse in a new philosophy of economics: inquiries into the basic concepts that cut across all economic systems, or help to shed light on the differences among them. (In conceptual depth and generality, and in the order of being, this level of discourse belongs first; although in my own inquiries, in the order of discovery, I came to it second.) The third discipline, which we will consider in the final section, has to do with special ethical dilemmas that arise *within* particular economic systems. For example, why are there firms or corporations in capitalist systems, and what is their nature and function? Should there be limits on the amount of compensation to chief executives of corporations? How did national planners set prices in existing socialist systems, and with what results?

(1) The study of basic concepts, (2) the study of comparative economic systems, and (3) the study of particular problems within systems—these are the three basic disciplines of a philosophy of economics.

At its second stage, a helpful philosophy of economics offers empirically testable hypotheses concerning the claims of rival systems, such as American capitalism vs. French and German social democracy, or vs. socialism such as that of Cuba, North Korea, and the pre-1989 Soviet Union. Each little boy and girl, Gilbert and Sullivan once sang, is born either a little liberal or a little conservative. When the hour strikes for these infants to begin to think critically, the choice of which economic system they intend consciously to support need no longer be based solely upon family upbringing and temperament. It can, in principle, be laid out in arguments amenable, one by one, to empirical falsifiability. One's initial beliefs, that is, can be submitted to systematic comparison with actual facts, so as to test their truth or falsehood.

To conduct such inquiries, a broad range of considerations forces the inquirer to stretch his mind to reach a high degree of philosophical clarity about as many as thirty or forty concepts that may not at first be clear in his head. These concepts are of varying sweep and breadth, and draw upon many different disciplines for their clarification. Simply to set them forth in an outline is to suggest the breadth and depth that an adequate philosophy of economics must reach. In digging deeper into more fundamental questions, the inquirer will certainly need to be clear about what he means by such basic terms as these:

- Time, history, progress, development (On time, Novak, 1982, chap. 5. On history and progress, Novak, 1982, chaps. 2–3. On development, Novak, 1990, chaps. 6–7; Novak, 1986, chap. 7; Novak, 1993, chap. 6; Novak, *Business as a Calling,* 1996, chaps. 4, 8–10; Novak, 1984, chaps. 7, 9, 10.);
- Family, association, organization, civil society, state (On family, Novak, 1982, chap. 8. On association, organization, and civil society, Novak, 1982, chaps. 2, 6; Novak, 1993, chap. 7; Novak, *Business as a Calling,* 1996, chaps. 6–7; Novak, 1999, chap. 4; Novak, 1984, Pt. 3; Novak, 1997, chap. 1. On state, Novak, 1982, Pt. 2; Novak, 1999, chap. 5.);
- Individual, person, liberty, action, habits, virtue (On individual, Novak, 1982, chap. 7. On person, Novak, 1990, chap. 4; Novak, 1993, epil.; Novak, 1989, chap. 1; On liberty, Novak, 1990; Novak, 1999; Novak, 1993, chap. 4. On action, Novak, 1997, chap. 3. On habits and virtue, Novak, 1990, chaps. 4–5; Novak, *Business as a Calling,* 1996, chaps. 5–7; Novak, 1993, chap. 3; Novak, 1989, 57–67, pp. 103–107; Novak, 1999, chap. 6; Novak, 1984, Pt. 3.);
- Insight, reflection, judgment, practical wisdom, intention, choice (Novak, *Business as a Calling,* 1996, chap. 5; Novak, 1982, chap. 5; Novak, 1999, Pt. 1.);
- Happiness, human flourishing, creativity and invention, common good, public interest, civility (On happiness and human flourishing, Novak, 1990, chaps. 6–7; Novak, 1986, chap. 7; Novak, 1993, chap. 6; Novak, 1996, *Business as a Calling,* chaps. 1, 4, 8–10; Novak, 1984, chaps. 7, 9, 10. On creativity and invention, Novak, 1996, *Business as a Calling,* chap. 6; Novak, 1986, chap. 5. On common good, Novak, 1989, chap. 1.);
- Equality of opportunity, equality under the law, equality of uniformity (Novak, 1982, chap. 11; Novak, 1997, pp. 108–13; Novak, "Inequality and Ideology," 1996.);
- Political liberty, economic liberty, moral cultural liberty (Novak, 1982, chap. 9; Novak, 1990, chaps. 8–9; Novak, 1986, chap. 10; Novak, 1999.);
- Objections against capitalism—political, economic, cultural, aesthetic (Novak, 1982, chap. 5; Novak, 1996, *Business as a Calling,* intro.; Novak, 1986, chap. 3; Novak, 1993, chap. 1.);
- Objections against socialism—political, economic, cultural, aesthetic (Novak, 1986, chap. 9; Novak, 1993, chap. 2; Novak, 1984, Pt. 2.);
- Error, misinformation, evil, sin, and irrationality (Novak, 1982, chap. 4; Novak, 1990, chap. 5; Novak, 1984, chap. 3.).

One will note that these are, as it were, *background* terms, belonging more to philosophy than to economics, and do not yet include such fundamental terms of economic discourse as *scarcity, abundance, demand, supply, general welfare, self-interest, full employment, inevitable trade-offs, economic reason, markets, enterprise,* and many others. Many arguments that *seem* to be about economic realities arise when individuals use these fundamental terms in different ways. Some of these usages are less plausible than others, and some are flat-out ill-informed. Much would be gained, then, by putting together a small handbook defining the correct usages of such terms and their interrelations, and exemplifying them in helpful ways. Isolating where disagreements actually lie is an enormous gain, since most disagreements are never defined clearly, but thrive in impenetrable fog.

I sometimes entertain the hope that, when confronted with evidence that disconfirms their earlier held expectations, reasonable persons will be able to change their minds. On the other hand, after the fall of socialism few on the Left admitted they had been wrong about socialist economics. Just the same, even when not everybody agrees, it is still good to have a reasonable method for clarifying *where* people do not agree. When that happens, fundamental political and economic disagreements are probably good for a free society.

THE THIRD LEVEL: FACING PARTICULAR QUESTIONS WITHIN CAPITALISM

When I first began this essay, I thought that in this section I would take up some particular problem within the capitalist system today, such as corporate compensation, the accounting scandals surrounding some six to ten major listed corporations (out of thousands of firms), debates about the minimum wage, or the like. All these questions deserve discussion. But I have been so struck by the sheer hostility against corporations voiced by many politicians in Washington, some journalists and TV pundits, and many professors on university campuses that it became unavoidably clear that a deeper issue must be addressed. Some years ago, when many intellectuals in the United States actually believed that some sort of socialism or social democracy was clearly the direction in which history was moving and *should* move, their contempt for capitalism was at least understandable. Socialism was the horse they put their money on. But after the utter collapse of socialist economies, one might have expected these cheerleaders to emerge a little chastened, a little more realistic about what can be done and why, and in that way come to some peace with economic reality. Instead, their underlying ire against capitalism, after being submerged for about a decade, has burst into the open again with a kind of hysterical passion and irrationality far less credible than before. Even commentators inclined to the Left have found it hard to see much coherence in the antiglobalization demonstrators who attack with violent rage big business, capitalism, and transnational corporations. In a less violent way, even Democratic centrists seem unable to resist lashing out against "the rich" and "big oil" and "business interests." The magnet placed beneath the grid of politics by Karl Marx still draws antibusiness particles leftward with the same old potency. Thus, in concluding these remarks I would like to draw attention to several current accusations against the capitalist systems by its university foes, particularly in departments of religion.

In a long essay on theology and economics, Joerg Rieger (2002) of the Perkins School of Theology at Southern Methodist University writes of the newly victorious capitalist system as though it were a disease, "expanding into the farthest regions of the globe and into most private realms of our lives" (p. 215). Rieger worries that this destructive disease invades people's worship (as in "refreshment of tired bodies and minds on Sunday morning"), concepts of faith (as in "faith-based institutions"), hope (as in the American determination to prevail after the first shock of Sept. 11, 2001), and charity (as in "compassionate conservatism"). Rieger is dismayed by the power of advertising, which is "geared towards reshaping our innermost desires and reaches levels of our humanity that we cannot control moralistically" (p. 218). He writes, "We are bombarded with thousands of images each day, all designed to shape our desires and to make us more perfect participants in the so-called 'free' market economy," and he rushes on in a panic verging on hysteria:

> With every breath we take we are integrated into the market, be it through the workplace, the way we relax, the way we shop, the way we save money, the way we plan for our retirement, the way we address social need, not to mention the influence of media and entertainment. During most of our working hours we are, therefore, more or less directly hooked up with the market economy. . . . [We are in a world] where even our best intentions and heroic actions are constantly being pulled into the vortex of the market. . . . Theology and the church—even where they try to resist—may be unconsciously shaped by the capitalist market economy. (p. 218)

Stop to think for a moment. It is not only under capitalism that economic concerns press on nearly everybody. Are not the gospels themselves redolent with the pastoral, rural economy of first-century Palestine? Are not the apostles and ordinary people preoccupied with plowing, seeding, harvesting, fishing, finding and preparing food, seeking places to sleep? In the Socialist countries under Communism, every minute of every day was shaped by standing in line, hardship, scarcity, and sensory deprivation. Under social democracy, fights over subsidies and privileges, handouts and prerogatives; a constant series of strikes for higher benefits or new privileges; and fears of high unemployment and dwindling reserves for old-age assistance, as the median age of the shrinking population base rises ever higher, color every minute of every waking day.

Scarcity and want are the human condition. Moreover, there is no evidence whatever that inequalities within capitalist societies exceed those in feudal society, or the distance between the *nomenklatura* in the Soviet Union and the impecunious peasants of the vast countryside outside Moscow. On the contrary, the Hungarian counts who dwelt in the great Castle of Spisska Podhradie in Central Slovakia inhabited realms of privilege far above the serfs who tilled the nobility's fields and cleaned their stables (such as my great-grandparents).

The rank of count was much farther removed from the common grasp than the currently successful sons and daughters of the American middle class, many of them born as poor as myself, who during their lifetimes become CEOs of America's largest companies.

Let me state this rebuttal another way. If Rieger wants to argue that the condition of the world's poor is worse today than, say, in 800 A.D. or 1250, or 1650, or 1880, or 1933, or 1976, he will have to demonstrate that assertion, not merely allude to it as a silent assumption. It can be shown without extraordinary effort that on practically every index of health—mortality, infant mortality, the elimination of certain destructive diseases and the discovery of cures for others, caloric intake, clean water, and care for the eyes and teeth—a growing proportion of the human population is better off under capitalist systems, on levels far beyond those even dreamed of in earlier systems. The same can be said for literacy, basic democratic freedoms, and elementary rights. Before capitalism, even kings and presidents were bled to death by unknowing doctors, and their easiest mode of transport was by horse, not an SUV.

Rieger (2002) describes capitalism as generating "a full-blown *repression* and the powers that cause it . . . The fate of people *on the underside* has to do with the *repressions* by which our so-called free economy operates. Economic expansion is built, for instance, on the vast availability of cheap labor" (p. 219, italics added). But Rieger will have to show that there is more cheap labor today, under capitalist systems, than there was in Egypt for the building of the pyramids, or in feudal Europe for the building of the castles, or among rural populations generally, in those regions where the growing season was short. (Bishop Berkeley commended early capitalism in Ireland for bringing indolent peasants into productive labor.) Is there greater cheap labor today under capitalism than there was in Communist Eastern Europe and China? Is there a higher proportion of unemployed people in social democratic Europe than in the capitalist United States today? It is invention, not cheap labor, that fires economic expansion—the invention of products never seen before such as computers and cell phones.

It is possible that Professor Rieger has not noted the rapid rise in economic prosperity in the nations of East Asia, in Chile, in Southern Europe, in Ireland, and increasingly in China and India since 1980. Extreme poverty in such regions, vast only fifty years ago, has been tremendously reduced, thanks to the spread of capitalist methods and conceptions. The capitalist economy is not, as he puts it, "expanding" because it does not help people, but because it does. Those capable of comparing it to alternative systems have come to recognize that it works far better than their current systems. It is expanding by desire and by imitation.

Professor Rieger (2002) denies that capitalism "and the desires connected with it are 'natural'" (p. 218). Reiger thinks that the allegation of "natural" springs from the vulgar desire of "keeping up with the Joneses," and that all people everywhere "want more stuff . . . a bigger car, a bigger house, and more money at the expense of everybody else" (pp. 218–19). But this is silly. What Adam Smith (1937) posited as two natural desires, important for economic development, but too humble to have been noted by earlier moral philosophers, are these: "the natural desire to improve one's condition" and "the natural desire to truck and barter." In other words, humans desire self-improvement, including economic self-improvement, and a cooperative spirit of voluntary and fair exchange. There are many examples of both of these natural desires in the Bible, not to say throughout the history of homo sapiens in all times and places. Markets, too, have been virtually universal and in the Bible are ubiquitous.

Thus, Rieger seems to have less than an accurate idea of what is distinctive about capitalism. It is not markets, nor private property, nor profits that are distinctive—all of which existed, even flourished, in precapitalist eras (such as the Biblical era). What is distinctive to capitalism *qua* capitalism is the organization of an economic system around the human mind—around invention, discovery, and the sort of enterprise that creates things that never existed before. In a capitalist economy, people do not need to get "more money *at the expense of everybody else* [italics added]," as Rieger (2002) falsely imagines. That was precisely the condition of the precapitalist, even premodern, mercantile economy, in which avarice was the besetting sin. In those days, wealth was limited, and anyone's acquisition of wealth necessarily deprived others, in a zero-sum game. In a capitalist economy, unprecedented amounts of new wealth are created that do not "take" from anybody else. On the contrary, new inventions increase the whole world's pool of wealth and distribute it more roundly to larger proportions of others than at any previous period of world history. That is precisely why so many of the formerly poor, including many of America's anticapitalists, are now middle class. From this highly favored position some can now rail against the system for not matching up their utopian views of the way a society ought to be arranged.

Professor Rieger (2002) asserts more than once in his essay that criticism of the capitalist system is stifled and that "no critique of the system is permitted" (p. 218). His entire career and those of scores of thousands of other intellectuals show that that claim is false. It is far rarer to meet a theologian in favor of capitalism—and for articulate, defensible reasons—than to meet dozens who are critical, even publicly disdainful, of it.[2]

Without elaborating, Rieger (2002) quotes without critical comment the opinion of a feminist theologian: "We middle-class North American Christians are destroying nature, not because we do not love it, but because of the way we live" (p. 215). *Destroying nature?* That is a highly improbable claim. Consider the ecology of North America itself. If we look at the ecology of North America in the year 1450, or 1650, or 1850, we would find large stretches of it were then

[2]In 1982, the IEA/Roper Center Theology Faculty Survey made clear that 37 percent of professors in theological schools want the United States to move in the direction of socialism; 36 percent thought Marxism consistent with membership in their denomination; 92 percent thought democratic socialism consistent; 70 percent think that U.S. multinational corporations hurt the Third World; 70 percent think the United States treats the Third World unfairly; 18 percent find the United States a force for ill in the world, and 25 percent find it only neutral.

Karl Zinsmeister reports in *The American Enterprise* (2002) that in the following university departments, the ratio of Democrats to Republicans is: Cornell University Economics 10/3, History 29/0, Political Science 16/1; Harvard University Economics 15/1, Political Science 20/1; Stanford University Economics 21/7, History 22/2, Political Science 26/4.

composed of inhospitable deserts, virtually uninhabitable and untamed plains, eroding mountains, and frequently poisonous streams (Johnson, 1977, p. 91). The ability of North America to sustain human life, and the average mortality of the people who inhabited North America, were by current standards very low.

As a matter of plain fact, modern North Americans have led the way to vastly improved health care, living conditions, and expectations of mortality, not only in North America but also in other parts of the world through the medicine, hygiene, and science that they have pioneered and eagerly shared with others. So what is one to make of the extreme claim that North Americans are responsible for "destroying" nature outside America's own national boundaries? That extreme claim is indefensible. Indeed, the opposite is closer to the truth. In some ways the ability of the earth to sustain human life (at an ever higher standard of quality) has been lifted to a higher level than at any prior period in history. A higher proportion of people are alive, living longer, and living better than ever before. Again, if crucially needed minerals and other "nonrenewable" resources were becoming scarcer, the laws of economics predict that they would be becoming more expensive. But the opposite is the case. In all but rare instances, precious resources are experiencing falling prices, compared with earlier years (Eberstadt, 2002).[3]

If Professor Rieger is receiving the average professorial wage for a tenured university position, and if in addition he earns a little money lecturing and writing, he stands no doubt in the top ten percent of all income earners in the United States.[4] His standing may be even higher if he is married and his wife also receives income. But it is clearly true that he does not consider making money the highest end of his life. Actually, in fact, a large majority of Americans do not. About sixty-four percent of American adults are working for income; about thirty percent of able-bodied persons between the ages of 18 and 65 are not working for income at all. Among the 139 million people employed in the United States, 24 million work for the *Fortune* 500 corporations, about 50 million are employed by businesses with less than 100 employees, and almost 10 million people are primarily self-employed. About 20 million work for government—federal, state, and local. About as many (author's estimate)—counting all teachers, researchers, medical professionals, directors, and staff—work for nonprofit organizations such as hospitals, clinics, libraries, museums, schools, universities, foundations, the Girl Scouts, the Sierra Club, and thousands of other nonprofit associations and activist groups. Less than half of all the employed work in the for-profit sector, creating the new wealth off of which the rest of us live.

And most of these, like my father, prefer time with family and a lower level of job commitment over chances for advancement that entail longer hours and continuous travel. Most prefer the kind of work that makes them happy to a

[3]In "Population Sense and Nonsense," *The Weekly Standard* (2002) Nicholas Eberstadt writes, "Despite the tremendous expansion of the international grain trade over the past century, for example, the inflation-adjusted, dollar-denominated international price of each of the major cereals—corn, wheat, and rice—fell by over 70 percent between 1900 and 1998."

[4]The IRS reports that the top 10 percent of all income earners in the United States earned above $92,144 per annum; the top 5 percent earned at least $128,336 per annum. See "Individual Income Tax Returns" (2002).

more demanding kind in which they could make more money. People ambitious for great wealth, or even for great achievement, are few. Indeed, long experience with college students shows that most students are quite content just to get by.

Furthermore, Professor Rieger's claim that Americans are peculiarly money driven must be set alongside Jacques Maritain's observation in *Reflections on America* (1958) that "the American people are the least materialist among the modern peoples which have attained the industrial stage" (pp. 28, 33). What is the evidence, either way?

Finally, it must be said that Rieger's description of Americans cringing under a deluge of seductive images (presumably from television) seems preposterous. Neither advertising gurus nor retailers feel anything like the omnipotence with which Rieger endows them. They sometimes experience abject failure and, most of the time, barely enough success to keep going. A great many highly touted products, like the Edsel, just die. True, some products are so good that they are smashing successes, but rarely is it the advertising alone that brings them their good fortune.

The bottom line is that many intellectuals are scaring themselves into extremist positions for which they must present empirical evidence. They do not have such evidence. They are misled by an inner antipathy for an economic system they do not show evidence of understanding, whether in itself or by just comparison with other systems. They seem to imagine some personal or perhaps collective vision of utopia, and compare capitalism and democracy to that vision while neglecting the existing economic and political alternatives. They also fail to notice a significant clue: the long, long lines of immigrants from all over the world. At any one time, millions of them are waiting for their visa applications to be processed, straining to enter into the very few dynamic capitalist and democratic systems of the world, precisely because those who enter such systems poor have a very high probability of escaping poverty within a half-dozen or so years. Democratic and capitalist countries are good for the poor. They are, in fact, the last best hope of the poor of the world.

CONCLUSION

While the philosophy of economics that I offer does not challenge the underlying foundations of the discipline, it serves to buttress a growing conviction that capitalism offers the best opportunity to improve the living conditions of the world's poor. In a word, those who are called to vocations in business have a great chance to swell the numbers of people around the world now exiting from poverty. Businessmen and women do this by means of the creative economic enterprises that will spring from their own imagination, discipline, sweat, intelligence, and hard work. Without taking money from anybody else, they are in a position to create new wealth never before seen, and to pay most of it out to workers, pensioners, shareholders, suppliers, transporters, and in good value to their customers. *Create and give!* That is not a bad motto for what capitalists are called to do. Be worthy of it.

Chapter 6

The Theology of Economics

Robert H. Nelson

ECONOMICS AND RELIGION IN AN INCREASINGLY SECULARIZED SOCIETY

A value-neutral economics can be of no real benefit to society. Thus, it is important that Christian economists assert themselves in the academy. Modern economics offers its own worldview, one that stands in sharp contrast to the Christian worldview. The dominant view of economics as value-free is difficult to defend when it is understood that economics is itself a religion—worshiping at the altar of free enterprise and submitting to the gospel of efficiency and growth. Arguing that any religion is value free ignores the reality that every religion offers its own value system.

It is a good idea sometimes to present one's conclusions at the beginning. Readers are not left wondering where one is going. I will use that approach now. I will start with an overall summary of my views on some of the key issues that have been addressed in this book. This also serves as a summary of views that I have developed in my two books that address the connections between economics and religion. *Reaching for Heaven on Earth* was published in 1991. The more recent, *Economics as Religion,* came out in 2001. I attempt to establish in these books that the ideas of economists and the development of the American economics profession are closely related to religious questions (see also Nelson 1994, 1995, 1997b, 1998b, and 2001a).

The rise of professional economics was a part of the general secularization of American society. It is not a coincidence that the rise of the economics profession dates to the progressive era. This was the time in American history when Harvard, Princeton, and other universities converted from their traditional religious orientations to instruction in the methods of scientific management. The rise of professional economics occured roughly simultaneously with the increasing marginalization of Christian religion in the arena of American public life. George Marsden talked about the marginalization in an earlier chapter. This theme is found in many of his writings. In effect, the university world abandoned Christian belief and converted to new forms of secular religion such as the American progressive "gospel of efficiency."

This may be more controversial, but I think that any economist, whether Christian or non-Christian, who actively participates in the current American economics profession is helping to advance the further marginalization of Christianity. I would say this, at least, with respect to the forms of Christianity that have historically been most influential and with respect to those with which most attendees of the 2002 conference at Baylor are associated. There has been a long conflict in the modern era between—as I would put it—secular religion and Christian religion. It seems to me that scholars have to make a choice. It is one or the other. Otherwise, it is like saying that you are a Christian and a Muslim simultaneously.

Now, this does not mean that all forms of religion have been marginalized with the rise of the economic profession—I am really saying just the opposite. Professional economics has been part of a broader spread of secular religion in American life. In fact, the economics profession is itself the priesthood of a powerful secular religion.

There are also other secular religions that do not have anything to do with economics. I recently discovered a book on *Psychology as Religion* (1994), written well before my own book on *Economics as Religion.* In my view, the greatest religious dynamism in American society in the twentieth century was associated with the rise of secular religions. Besides economic religion, I would include the secular religion of environmentalism—in fact, the environmental gospel is doing very well these days. I have also written about the religious side of environmentalism (1990, 1993, 1995, 1997a, 1997c, 1998a, 2003) and am now thinking of writing a book on this subject.

Although they are secular religions, both the economic and environmental gospels derive many of their core messages from the Judeo-Christian tradition. In this sense, one might even say that Christianity today is thriving in public life. It is just that this "Christianity" is operating in disguise as economics or as environmentalism—or as one or another of the various forms of secular ideology. It does not make any difference that many current economists and environmentalists are not even aware that they are heirs to the Christian tradition and to the teachings of Christian theology. The modern age seems to have been characterized by widespread efforts to repackage Christianity as science, reflecting the tendency of many modern intellectuals to find an authority in "Science" that earlier eras had found in God.

From one perspective, it is possible that Christianity is once again being reshaped and reworked. This has happened several times over the history of the past 2,000 years. It started off with the synthesis of St. Paul, which brought together the New and the Old Testaments and created a religion outside the Jewish fold. In later centuries Christian theology was significantly reworked by Augustine, Thomas Aquinas, and others to reconcile Christian teachings with Greek philosophy. Possibly Christians are in yet another period where a grand synthesis is being improvised and new forms of Christian religion are in the process of being born. This inevitably involves wide confusion and many dead ends, but it may eventually lead to something that will be of great importance in religious history. It may involve some kind of fundamental synthesis of modern ideas—associated with claims to truth derived from science—with more historic Christian beliefs and theology. The modern era itself attempted such a synthesis, but these efforts increasingly look unpersuasive.

If this interpretation is correct, perhaps society is really at the beginning of a new postmodern era. Maybe the postmodern project is really about a revival of Christianity but in a new form that is better suited to a reconciliation of modern scientific truth with traditional Christian truth. In this view, the modern era itself perhaps was simply a long hiatus in the development of a more coherent Christian theology. It seems to me that we are living today, in general, at a time of great religious ferment. The Nobel-Prize-winning economist from the University of Chicago, Robert Fogel, has recently written that the United States is experiencing yet another of the great religious awakenings of American history. Religious revival today is occurring partly within traditional religion but also partly in secular forms outside traditional religion. Maybe America is seeing today the birth spasms of a new era of postmodern religion.

Now, why are such speculations potentially so important? It is because the subjects of economics and the activities of the economics profession (as a new priesthood) are playing central roles in this postmodern process of theological reassessment.

FROM MY YOUTH TO GRADUATE STUDY AT PRINCETON

At this point, I want to switch gears and offer some explanation of how I came to these views. Relating the broader themes to some of my own personal background helps to make things more concrete. The views just expressed are a process of continuing evolution that goes back at least to the time I was a student in college.

The Culture of My Youth

Unlike many of attendees of the Baylor conference, I was brought up in a family of true believers in secular religion. My great-grandfather was a Protestant minister in the Swedish Evangelical Covenant Church in the United States, and his daughter, my grandmother, was very devout. As a minister, my great-grandfather believed that one should educate a person enough to read the Bible, but no more education than that. If a person went past the eighth grade, he was more likely to endanger his faith than to be benefited spiritually. My great-grandfather may have been right from his perspective because that is what happened in the case of my father. He went off to college—this was around World War II—and became part of a generation convinced of the truths of science and of economic religion. He also became a college professor of economics and business administration for 20 years. So he was one of the great wave of academics that George Marsden speaks of who were instrumental in secularizing the American university in the twentieth century.

That was the environment of my youth. There was an assumed automatic belief in the power of economic ideas and economic progress to reshape the world for the better. All this was pretty much taken for granted—it was not necessary to develop an explicit "economic theology." When something seems so obviously true, there is less need for a formal theology or the development of a precise logical explanation. In any case, that is where I started from theologically—a true believer in economic progress in my youth. My attitudes were not unusual. A faith in progress at that time was pervasive in American society; one might call it the religion of the American welfare and regulatory state (the official public "church" of America) of the twentieth century. *The New York Times,* the major television networks, and many other contemporary opinion leaders preached this theology nonstop—that conditions in the world and its future prospects are explained by economic phenomena.

Economic religion may not be a formal theology, but presidents run for office on the basis of who can stimulate the fastest rate of growth (remember "It's the economy, stupid"?). When the media wants to say that something is "good," it says that it will "improve the productivity" of the American economy. Since the progressive era, "efficient" and "inefficient" have been the secular substitutes for the "good" and "evil" of Christian religion. Indeed, the progressive faith has been labeled by several historians as the "gospel of efficiency," and economists have carried the professional mantle of efficiency in the second half of the twentieth century.

There was not much space left in my religious thinking—or in that of many other Americans—for traditional Christianity. I went to Sunday school fairly regularly but, truthfully, almost nothing sunk in. When I became more interested later in the history of Christian theology, it required a new start in self-education.

Embrace of the "Gospel of Efficiency"

Now, why are economic progress and economic efficiency so important that they took the place of Christian religion for me and so many other Americans in the twentieth century? One way to put this is to say that economic progress can save the world. I would not have put it that way in my youth, but I never-the-less believed in those days that economic progress is in essence the path to heaven on earth.

Why would anyone think that? At this point, it may help to use some more explicitly religious language. Among the fundamental religious questions, the cause of sin is certainly central. The Bible says that the cause of sin in the world is to be found in the Fall in the Garden of Eden. In economic religion, however, the source of human sinfulness is much closer to hand; evil actions have environmental causes and are directly attributable to the economic circumstances in which a person lives.

If someone behaves badly, according to economic theology, the explanation must lie in material deprivation. If given a choice between feeding their children and lying, cheating, stealing, or maybe even killing, many people will choose the latter. This is the secular version of original sin—as you might call it.

For example, what are wars about? Many people have said that war is basically the product of struggle for access to natural resources and other material inputs into production. Recently, I read a report that illustrates very well the perspective of economic theology (Chapman, 1995). It was in a scientific magazine and was a report about chimpanzees and how they behave in different environmental circumstances. When the rainfall is good and there is abundant food available to them, the chimpanzees behave peacefully and benevolently. However, if the weather is bad and if their food supplies run short, the chimpanzees end up squabbling, fighting, and stealing among themselves. This is based on actual field research. The empirical result observed in this research is actually close to the core assumption of economic theology. It is assumed that, after living many millennia at the edge of survival, and with an evolutionary struggle for survival of the fittest, human beings have come to behave much the same way as chimpanzees. They may have a veneer of civilization, but it is a thin veneer. Underneath, people are like the chimpanzees, willing to do what is necessary to survive—whatever the Ten Commandments might say.

This is the fundamental premise of economic theology, and it is a premise that has been very widely shared in at least the Western world over the last 150 years. It can be found, for example, at the core of Marxist "religion" and the Marxist idea that all of history is shaped by a class struggle centered on competition for material resources and for material advantage. This class struggle shapes everything in society, including even such "opiates" as Christian religion. If one accepts this view, it has radical implications. If human beings could somehow solve the economic problem, they could then also solve the problem of sin in the world. If they could somehow achieve a condition of total material abundance by human actions, they could actually bring an end to human sinfulness on earth. That is to say human beings may now have the capacity to save themselves by their own scientific and economic intelligence.

There is no need for God in this vision. It is human thinking and human effort that reach heaven on earth—the equivalent in secular religion of reaching the millennium for Christianity. There are other radical implications. The Roman Catholic priesthood and the Protestant ministry can now fade into history. If the path to heaven on earth is economic, it will be economists—not priests or ministers—who know the correct path to the salvation of the world. Economists will be the ones who have the knowledge to eliminate material scarcity in the world, and this will be the means by which evil actions will finally be abolished in human affairs. People do not need to read the Bible any more. They do need to read, however, economics textbooks and other explanations of the requirements for economic progress in the world. The members of the economics profession will have as their charge to conduct economic research and to communicate the results of their scientific discoveries to the American public. In this way, they will play their essential part in reaching heaven on earth.

Graduate Study in Economics at Princeton

When I entered graduate school in economics at Princeton, in 1966, I would say that I already believed much of the above. However, it was all implicit rather than explicit. I would never have put it in precisely those terms. You might say that "economic religion" was more of a folk religion than a well developed theology. Still, I knew that I was being trained in graduate school to go out into the world to spread the gospel of economic progress. I might, for example, end up in a job at the World Bank (as several of my fellow graduate students in economics in fact did) and then work to show the poor nations of Africa, Asia, and Latin America how they might join the modern world—based in the end on their ability to learn how to follow the economic model of the United States and Europe. The many economists who went to work for the World Bank in the second half of the twentieth century were the missionaries, as it appears to me now, of the religion of economic progress.

It was not only Princeton and its economics graduate program, of course. The same thinking could be found at other leading economics departments such as MIT and Stanford—even at Chicago, which was out of the mainstream in many other respects. The field of economics was emerging in those days as preeminent among the social sciences. Economists were the only ones, for example, who had the direct ear of the President of the United States through the Council of Economic Advisors. However, the other social sciences, the schools of resource management, the schools of business administration—in fact most of the "professional" schools of the university world—were committed to a similar agenda. The university had become the new seminary for modern secular religion. The actual Christian seminaries survived at Princeton Theological Seminary. The seminary students were pulled out of the university mainstream and isolated in their own school as a reminder of the past.

Princeton students were in economics graduate school to learn the true knowledge and to gain the valid tools and abilities to save the modern world. I heard quite a bit during the Baylor conference about economics treating people as crassly self-interested. I think that this is a serious misreading of what professional economics has been about. Economics fundamentally has been about giving people collectively the instruments of their own social salvation. It might happen that the pursuit of self-interest can serve this goal—as in making a market system workable. But encouraging self-interest is not the end in itself. It is part of some larger and much more benevolent vision, a vision of human redemption here on earth. That is what brought many of the graduate students to the Princeton economics department (not that the other students ever used such explicitly religious language).

Of course, there were also fellow graduate students in economics who were mainly looking for comfortable jobs and a nice salary. Being a college professor is a pleasant life. Such motives probably affected at least somewhat everyone who was there, including me. But I would say only a minority were in graduate school just for the job prospects. One of my classmates (and a personal friend as well) was James Heckman, who is now a professor of economics at the University of Chicago and won the Nobel Prize in economics in 2000. Heckman's personal background was somewhat like my father's. He had been brought up in a devout home and then left Christianity as an adult for economics. This kind of conversion from traditional religion of one's youth to secular religion as an adult was widespread among academics in the twentieth century.

Heckman also was (and still is) legendary among economists for his zeal, his enthusiasm for hard work, and his dedication to economic give-and-take. Knowing him personally, one would never say he was doing it for personal profit alone. Like a lot of other people at Chicago, he exhibits an obvious missionary zeal for what he would probably describe as the "true scientific enterprise" of economics. Milton Friedman is another good example of the Chicago tendency toward a missionary form of behavior, although Friedman (unlike Heckman) preaches his religious truths of economics in a free-market version.

I have to say that I find Friedman to be virtually a walking contradiction. He talks about the power of self-interest in the world, but this apparently does not apply to his own behavior either in reality or in his own characterization of his life "mission." If people are so self-interested, you have to wonder who Friedman expects will be reading and profiting from his own writings. I am confident, in fact, that Friedman expects his readers, like himself, to be "seekers after truth" who are willing to make personal sacrifices of time and effort to learn the path of economic efficiency. Of course, this is not the model of individual behavior of economic theory. The economic man of economic theory, it seems to me, would have no interest in reading Friedman's writings and would not be interested in saving anyone but himself.

So Friedman is writing for people who, it would seem, have to violate in their own lives some of the basic assumptions of his writings. Perhaps Friedman is thinking implicitly that a modern priesthood can be found that will behave differently than ordinary people who are concerned mainly with their own self-advancement. This modern priesthood, unlike ordinary people but like the medieval Catholic priesthood, should exhibit an altruistic commitment to the greater common good of society.

DOUBTS ABOUT THE RELIGION OF ECONOMICS

Poverty and Lyndon Johnson's War

So this was my graduate education in economics. It may be helpful to give some concrete examples of economic religion in practice. When I was in graduate school in the 1960s, some of America's most important cities had recently burned in riots. There was a great concern in American society for the problems of the poor. Lyndon Johnson declared a general war on poverty. I would argue that the premises of economic religion underlay much of the thinking about and the proposed policy solutions to American poverty in those days.

First, there was a core assumption that poverty is a social problem. The poor in inner cities commit crimes, have high illegitimacy rates, become drug abusers, and have other individual maladies because of their broader economic circumstances. It is a simple diagnosis. The poor are poor because they have been oppressed by their environment. If all this is true, then there is also a simple solution. At least in concept, society should be able to eliminate poverty by changing the economic environment of the poor. If the poor simply have more money, for example, they will no longer have the financial need to commit crimes. In fact, Milton Friedman (1962) proposed the negative income tax as the obvious solution to poverty. Another social scientist, White House advisor Patrick Moynihan, tried to convince Richard Nixon of the idea (Hodgson, 2000). It was all very much a part of the thinking of the times. The "poverty problem" was simply to find an efficient way to transfer money to the poor without creating negative disincentives for work effort.

Of course, we know now that by and large this approach did not work. The war on poverty did not solve the problem on poverty. In fact, crime rapidly went up almost simultaneously with pouring more and more money into inner-city areas. Overall, the country spent a very large amount of money and put a very large amount of human effort into solving the problem of poverty, much of it based on the assumptions of economic religion. In the end, given the wide failures of these efforts, it is hard to avoid the conclusion that economic religion must have ignored some fundamental part of the problem of poverty.

By now, there is a great deal of frustration. In fact, one now hears about faith-based welfare programs. It is a sign of the increasing presence of a new (or perhaps we should say old) religion. There are echoes in the policy debate of more traditionally Christian ways of thinking about poverty. The poor may be poor because they are sinners. To eliminate poverty, one needs first to save the souls of the poor. More missionary efforts, not more money, are the real solution to poverty. Poverty programs may need to follow in the path of programs like Alcoholics Anonymous.

In order to reduce poverty, some might even argue that more people must be "born again." That would obviously be a radical departure for public policy. It also shows some of the problems society may face in the future. How is it possible to use public funds to promote a process in which the goal is that more people should be born again? At some point, might America have to abolish the very idea of separation of church and state?

Saving China Economically

There are other areas in which economic religion has played a central role in influencing recent public policy. In U.S. foreign affairs, for example, consider policies toward China. The United States is seeking to promote economic development as part of a long-term process of bringing China fully into the modern age. Yet the process has a long way to go. China in many ways is not a very nice place—there are tight limits on personal freedom, widespread executions, and in general a degree of tight social control over the individual that many Americans would find oppressive.

The implicit premise of the China policy is that economic development in that nation will change these objectionable features. A richer China would be more democratic, more peaceful, more respectful of human rights, and would become a good citizen in the world community of nations. That is basically an expression of economic theology. Material advance leads to moral improvement as well as more goods and services. Like the remedy for inner cities, the solution to poverty is to be found in scientific understanding of economic processes. By improving the economic conditions of the poor, whether in American cities or in China, the result will be the abolition of "evil actions" in the world.

However, what if our assumptions about China turn out to be wrong—as they turned out to be at least partly wrong in America's own antipoverty programs? The United States is working hard today to make China rich and powerful in the future. If its behavior as a nation does not also change for the better, the United States may be confronted with a large, powerful, and potentially antagonistic force in international affairs—a force in significant part of its own making. Thus, for China policy, the validity or lack of validity of the premises of economic religion represents an extremely important issue. Will economic progress "save" China?

Suppose that the United States rejects the idea that economic progress brings corresponding improvements in individual and collective behavior. U.S. policymakers might then have to rethink their entire China policy. Perhaps they would have to try to develop a "faith-based" China policy. Conceivably, it could involve sending new Christian missionaries to China—instead of economic development experts from the World Bank.

September 11, 2001

Another related example of economic theology occurred in the aftermath of the September 11th attacks on the World Trade Center in New York. Right after September 11, many people were greatly concerned to try to understand the explanation for such terrorist behavior—the reasons for this extraordinary manifestation of the presence of evil in the world. Probably the most common explanation heard in the United States was that Islamic terrorism is a product of economic frustration in the Middle East. The explanation for Arab hatred of America is to be found in poverty—this time among the poor in Egypt, Pakistan, and other nations. Once again, "original sin" was seen as having an economic cause.

The solution must then also be economic. There will have to be economic progress in the Middle East in order to bring about a new social order. The United States needs to increase foreign aid, to send more economic experts to Indonesia, to rebuild Afghanistan economically, and so forth. If poverty in these places could be reduced and eventually eliminated, the divisions between the Christian West and the Islamic world would also be undermined. Such thinking offers a graphic illustration of the application of the tenets of economic theology to a pressing world issue.

However, once again, economic theology might have it all wrong. Indeed, the facts do not fit the theology very well in this case. Osama bin Laden came from one of the richest families in Saudi Arabia. Most of the airplane hijackers were better-off, or at least more better-off than most other people in the nations where they were born. Many of the hijackers had lived long periods in the West; they chose consciously to reject Western values, in effect a religious choice independent of economic circumstances. In order to change their behavior, economic methods would not seem to be of much help. If there is any possibility of having an influence on Islamic terrorists, it would seem to lie in some form of religious persuasion, or in the direct application of force.

Maybe a central goal of American foreign policy should be to establish a new religious conversation with Islamic societies. Perhaps there needs to be a theological discussion of the possibility that the theology of Islam includes some elements that work to promote violent tendencies. Perhaps official U.S. policy should be working harder to show that bin Laden is a heretic—not a Christian heretic but a heretic in terms of the fundamental ideas of Islamic religion itself. Instead of promoting economic progress, the leading instrument of American foreign policy may have to be found in theological conversion and argument. Once again, public policy and theology seem to be coming together.

LIFE AFTER PRINCETON AND GROWING DOUBTS ABOUT THE FAITH

To return to my individual journey, I did eventually get a Ph.D. in economics at Princeton in 1971. I was brought up in economic religion but, as you have probably gathered by now, I am an economic apostate at present. I doubt that economic progress will save the world. My first step in turning away from the professional economic mainstream was in the early 70s. It was not as much a question in those days of the specific tenets of economic religion as of the basic economic methods that I had just been taught in graduate school. They simply seemed to me to be too formal and thus were barren and empty of insight. Economic theorizing was too mathematical, in many cases amounting to little more than a fancy tautology. Much of the time economists were taking simple, even rather obvious, ideas and putting them in a technical jargon. Based on the fact that they spoke in mathematics, economists then made claims that "economic science" was on a par with the physical sciences.

By the early 1970s, I had concluded that this was mostly false pretenses. I decided to get out of academic economics because I was not comfortable teaching something that I did not believe. By 1975, I ended up in the Office of the Secretary of the U.S. Department of the Interior in Washington, D.C. I worked in the Office of Policy Analysis, a small in-house think tank populated heavily by other economists. I was not a traditional government bureaucrat, however. In fact, I am here now because I had a great deal of freedom at the Interior Department to write and think about the big picture. I also was able to watch government administration at work, to meet the political players, and in general to see the policy-making process firsthand. Although I did not have any final decision-making authority as a staff person, it was a fascinating place to be. In some ways, it was my real education, teaching me more about the way the world really works than I had learned at Princeton.

I stayed at the Interior Department until 1993, when I returned to the academic world with an appointment to my current position at the University of Maryland. It is in the public policy school entitled the School of Public Affairs. I would probably not be able to get a job today at most economics departments in the United States. I majored in mathematics as an undergraduate at Brandeis University from 1962 to 1966. However, I have not done anything mathematical in economics since the early 1970s. In any case, the experience of working at the Interior Department forced me to rethink the role of economics in the world and the best ways of doing economic analysis (Nelson, 1987).

When I arrived at the Interior Department, I did not really think that the economics I had recently learned in graduate school was going to be very helpful. However, I did then—and still do—think that certain basic economic ideas can be very powerful. It is important to understand supply and demand in thinking about many policy issues. I also expected to find that interest groups would be important in government decision-making and that outside interests would often drive the policy results at the Interior Department. In retrospect, all of these expectations turned out to be at least partially true.

I was surprised when I arrived at the department, however, to see the extent to which the policy-making process there was often grounded in clashes of social values. Policy-making often was not technical, it often was not interest-group driven; rather, in many cases it was basically a fierce fight about competing visions of the world. As I would say today, my greatest surprise at the Interior Department was to discover how important religions—often but not always secular religions—turned out to be in policy-making.

However, there is a longstanding fear in American society of any strong expression of religious emotion and conflict in public. Religion ranks with sex and money as private subjects that people try to keep out of the public arena. As a result, the religious conversation is often pushed underground. Basic disagreements about social values are obscured by a large overlay of technocratic jargon—often provided by economists. Social values may be embedded in the technocratic language, but it requires a translator to reveal these values. Most economists are reluctant to provide the translation; in fact, many of them deny that core values are even being actively expressed. However, for those able to decipher economic and other allegedly scientific code, it is apparent that government decisions very often are being driven by an underlying clash of social values—or, as I increasingly came to believe, by an underlying clash of religious beliefs. I had not understood this before arriving at the Interior Department, but theological debate and symbolism were where the real action frequently lay.

THE DEPARTMENT OF RELIGION

If I had known more about the Interior Department, I might have been less surprised. (And I should also acknowledge that there might have been more of a useful role for technical economic analysis at other government departments such as the Treasury Department.) While I was working at the Interior Department, I sometimes joked that it was really the Department of Religion of the U.S. government. The Interior Department managed the secular shrines of American life. The department was responsible for the Lincoln Memorial. It oversaw the Gettysburg battlefield, the Grand Canyon, and Yosemite. Wilderness areas on federal lands were modern churches—the most inspiring cathedrals of the time for many people. The Interior Department administered the Endangered Species Act, which one Secretary of the Interior, Bruce Babbitt, once called the new Noah's Ark for modern times (Nelson, 1996).

Interior dams such as Hoover Dam or Grand Coulee Dam were no longer in fashion by the 1970s, but at the time of their construction they had also been modern cathedrals, inspirational places for the worship of the modern god of human progress. They symbolized the human ability to control nature, which was seen by the great majority of Americans as a positive good until the 1960s.

It was important as a top official in the Interior Department to know how to pay proper respect to all these leading symbols of the American civil religion.

Given the importance of the Interior Department's religious role, policy making there took on a new meaning. It could be, in essence, an exercise in theology. Christianity has a field of applied Christian ethics. At the department, employees were often forced to be students of applied secular religious ethics. For example, how many wilderness areas of spiritual inspiration do the American people need? It was like asking the question how many churches are needed. One public policy issue recently involved the permanent placement of rock pitons—used by mountain climbers—in wilderness areas. Should they, or should they not, be allowed in a wilderness area? Mountain bikes, for example, are prohibited even when they are not motorized. Such issues cannot be resolved by economics; it is really a matter of making a "theological" judgment. Would, or would not, the permanent placement of these pitons desecrate the wilderness values of the area?

When I arrived at the Interior Department in 1975, it was the heyday of the environmental movement. The first Earth Day had been held in 1970; a wave of environmental legislation moved through Congress throughout the 1970s. I call it the "environmental revolution" of the 1970s. However, I was somewhat surprised to find that I was in frequent disagreement with environmentalists. It was at this point that I began to think that environmentalism is like economics; they are both forms of secular religion. In fact, compared with economists, many environmentalists are less defensive about underlying religious inspiration. Some are even quite explicit and argue that the long-term success of the environmental cause in the United States depends on a religious conversion in American society—away from social values like consumerism.

Joseph Sax, a leading environmental lawyer in the United States, wrote a book in defense of the national park system—called *Mountains without Handrails* (1980). Sax stated approvingly that the environmental movement is filled with "secular prophets, preaching a message of secular salvation" (p. 104) for American society. The purpose of the national park system is to provide spiritual inspiration in a new message for mankind. John Muir founded the Sierra Club in 1892 and was a leader of the movement for preservation of nature in the early twentieth century. Muir often wrote explicitly in religious terms. For him, a wilderness was a place to be in closer contact with God. In a wilderness (Muir, 1968), as he said, a person can encounter the actual handiwork of God—in effect, it was a piece of the original Creation. That is why it is so important to preserve wilderness areas; otherwise, people would not have anything left of the original Creation on earth. It would be much worse than losing the Sistine Chapel: that was painted by Michelangelo, a mere human being. God is not literally in the wilderness (that would be the heresy of pantheism), but a person can find in the wilderness the very artwork of God.

Organized environmental groups today are not usually as explicit about all this as Muir in his day. Current environmental activists know that it could be somewhat awkward to employ such overtly religious language in a general public setting. Nevertheless, in their fund-raising solicitations, and in many other internal activities, members of the environmental movement often speak in directly moral and religious terms. They lament the "rape" of the land; the old growth forests are said to be a "new Eden"; natural objects are being "murdered"; people are called to "environmental witness"; and so forth. Society must stop "playing God" with the natural world. I could go on and on with examples of religious language from the environmental movement.

ECONOMIC RELIGION VERSUS ENVIRONMENTAL RELIGION

When I first encountered this religious side of environmentalism in the 1970s at the Interior Department, I found it somewhat troubling. Partly, I suppose, it was a challenge to my general secularism. It was obvious to me that many environmentalists were new fundamentalists, but they were much more politically powerful and more directly engaged in the public arena than traditional Christian fundamentalists. It also seemed to me that the political activism of environmentalists raised difficult questions of the separation of church and state. Maybe we were discriminating; the traditional Christian fundamentalists were being kept out, but environmental fundamentalists were being offered top government jobs in the Carter administration to put their religious beliefs into practice.

I suppose that I also recognized that environmentalists in many cases were challenging my own faith in the idea of economic progress. It was not a very strong faith, but it was still there. Many environmentalists seemed to think that progress really ought to be defined as "regress." If an economist thought that economic progress was the salvation of the world, the same progress for many environmentalists seemed to be the path to the destruction of the world.

Whatever the moral verdict, however, it is hard to see any way one could stop economic progress. Six billion people on earth have to be fed, sheltered, and clothed. Hunter-gatherer times, even if superior in some ways for human beings and other creatures of the world, could not offer much of relevance to the current human condition.

Moreover, economic progress has been a wonderful benefit to the people alive today—at least in the developed world. Populations live better in matters of food, communications, transportation, and medical care than even the kings and queens of a few hundred years ago. It is almost miraculous, and certainly most people three hundred years ago would never have predicted it. This may not go on forever—it is a hard argument to resolve definitely the "sustainability" of the current condition—but it is foolish to deny the current benefits. Too many environmentalists seem to me to be hopeless romantics. As society saw in the twentieth century, romantic impulses gone wrong (communism and fascism as the leading examples) could yield the worst outcome of all.

BECOMING AN "ECONOMIC THEOLOGIAN"

At first, I was not very articulate about the character of the religious tension that I was observing between economists and environmentalists. This kind of subject had certainly never come up for discussion in my studies in economics graduate school. I knew that professional economics felt religious and often exhibited a certain religious dogmatism. In their irrelevance to the real world, formal economic writings in the professional journals were reminiscent of old-fashioned scholasticism in the medieval period. However, I had not really addressed the question in my own mind of the actual religious content of economics. I also had not attempted to define in any explicit way the religious differences between the economic and environmental ways of thinking about the world.

Eventually, however, I began to feel the urge to think more seriously about these types of questions. If there were two strong sets of value judgments being expressed, where did these values come from? In the case of economics, this forced me to think about the implicit values expressed in economic arguments. Maybe economics was a religion in more than simply a metaphorical or sociological way. It began to dawn on me that perhaps economics offered an actual theology in the same sense that Christianity is grounded in a theology—that it had its own economic version of original sin.

Of course, "economic theology" requires certain assumptions that go beyond understanding the laws of an economic system. The idea that economic scarcity is the root of all evil in the world is not, strictly speaking, even an economist's idea. However, implicitly, as I explain further in my two books on the subject, economists do make this assumption in much of their work. Without it, economists would not be able to reach many of their most important policy conclusions.

Eventually, in 1986, I received a government fellowship to go to the Brookings Institution for a year. Brookings fortunately did not ask many questions about my intended course of study. If I had said that I wanted to write on the relationship between economics and religion, the people at Brookings might have said to try another place. In any case, at the Brookings Institution I wrote the first draft of a book that eventually came out in 1991 as *Reaching for Heaven on Earth: The Theological Meaning of Economics.* As I was working out my own thinking there, I described in explicit terms the premises and logic of economic theology. I have already described the core ideas above: the source of sin is economic scarcity; society can thus eliminate sin in human affairs by eliminating scarcity; economic progress can therefore bring heaven on earth. Economics, as it now seemed, was a disguised offering of some of the principal messages of Christianity—or a new Christian heresy, as some others might say. Heresies, it is said, are most dangerous to the faith when they represent only a limited departure from its core tenets.

I also argued in *Reaching for Heaven on Earth* that different economic schools had different ideas about the correct route of economic progress. Remarkably, the different ideas about the workings of economic progress mirror older controversies among competing forms of Christian theology. As I argued, most American economists were heirs to a Christian tradition that found its high points in the history of the Roman Catholic Church. Economists, like Roman Catholic theologians, believed in a rational world. Economists claimed they were studying scientific laws of economics, but their reasoning was reminiscent of the Roman Catholic treatment of natural law. In effect, economics offered an old-fashioned, natural-law understanding of the world, disguised as a modern, positivist understanding that claimed to be analogous to the physical sciences. Finally, professional economics served as the religion of the American welfare and regulatory state, which was hierarchically organized and centered in Washington, as the Roman Catholic Church was hierarchical and centered in Rome.

However, there were some schools within economics that were more Protestant in their basic understanding of the world. For such economists, the world is less rational, less controlled by human decision-making, and more a reflection of the sinful and depraved character of human beings since the Fall in the Garden of Eden. Marxism is the best example of a Protestant economics. But, of course, Marxism was never much of a factor in American economics. Strangely enough, America was founded by Puritans and other old-fashioned Protestants. But little of the original "doom and gloom" Protestantism survived in the economic theology of modern America.

To the extent there was a Protestant school of economics in the United States, it tended to be associated with University of Chicago economists. An economist such as Frank Knight—the founder of the Chicago school—might exhibit some clear Protestant tendencies in his economic thinking. Knight, for example, doubted that any real progress of a moral character could be achieved in the world by improvements in the economic environment. However, with the exception of Knight's follower James Buchanan, few other American economists showed similar skeptical and pessimistic tendencies of thought. Americans are by nature optimists, and the success of economists has reflected their ability to offer supporting arguments for this.

A CHRISTIAN ECONOMICS?

Given the central theme of the Baylor conference, and since I am close to the end of this essay, I will offer a few remarks about the possibilities for a new "Christian economics." It would be a substitute for scientific economics, recognizing that any system of economic thought will reflect some powerful value judgments. It might make sense, therefore, to develop a body of economic thinking that explicitly reflects a Christian set of values. If not Christian values, economists will reflect some other values—even when they refuse to put these values explicitly on the table. There can be no value-neutral economics of any great interest to society.

But a Christian economics would not only be about different values that have to be taken on faith. Christianity has been historically about establishing truth. It says in the Bible that "the truth will set you free." Science challenged Christianity by seeming to be able to make more accurate and powerful truth statements. A new approach to scientific economics will have to challenge this development. It will be important to show that introducing Christian ideas and Christian themes will produce a better understanding of economic truth. Max Weber, for example, showed how the theology of a religion could be central to the workings of an economic system. It might also be the case that a true belief in a religion is a more accurate predictor of personal happiness ("utility" in the jargon of economics) than the amount of goods and services that a person consumes. It has already been demonstrated by statistical research that religious people on average experience better personal health than nonreligious people. Similar studies could be made about levels of individual happiness.

Here is one example of what a new Christian economics might be. You could study the effects of religious belief or of religious conversion on the likelihood of a person escaping from poverty. You might gather a sample of 1,000 people who are living in poverty, and then follow this group for five years. Some of the people would be religious, or would have religious conversions, and others would not. Using econometric and other statistical methods, the effect of religion on the probability of an individual escaping from poverty could be estimated. It would also be useful to compare the effects of religion in this regard with the effects of other strategies that have been employed to try to help people escape from poverty. For example, a study might be done of religious conversion in terms of impact on future poverty, as compared with spending six months in a job-training program. Benefit-cost ratios might be developed, taking into account the costs of conversion and the costs of the job training.

In a more detailed analysis, one might also consider the impacts of different forms of religion. A study might assess the economic improvement of people over the five years who converted to the Baptist faith, versus other people who converted to the Mormon faith. Among those living in poverty at the beginning of the study, one might ask whether the members of one religious group, for example, tend to escape poverty more rapidly than the other. In Latin America, it is said that the most entrepreneurial and economically successful citizens today are likely to be found among recent converts to Protestantism in that region.

There is much contemporary discussion in the social sciences of the idea of social capital. A Christian economist perhaps might work with others to attempt to develop more operational measures of social capital using indicators of trust and other appropriate factors. One might then ask the question, Does a population of religious believers in the one faith, or in another faith, tend to generate a higher level of social capital? Another question might be to ask how these religious believers compare in this regard with a population of atheists. Does a group of Buddhists have a high level of social capital as compared with a similar group of Christians (or Muslims)?

Another form of Christian economics might involve a redefinition of the goals of the economic analysis. When a current economist considers the goal of efficiency, the analysis is conducted in terms of increasing the total production of goods and services that enter into gross national product. However, perhaps the goal of public policy should be to increase the overall sense of community in America. A Christian economist might examine various government policies in terms of the effectiveness, not in promoting a higher GNP, but in promoting the sense of community in American life. It might be possible to undertake forms of cost-effectiveness analysis in terms of advancing the goal of community. Does policy A advance the sense of community in American life as much per unit of dollar spending as policy B advances community? It is conceivable that at some point in the future *The American Economic Review* will be publishing some articles of this kind.

Another area for study might be the effectiveness of different forms of training for the ministry (an analysis of "Christian job training," as it might be called). A Christian economist could study whether church ministers who have formal theological training serve their congregations more successfully than ministers who are self-taught. In any case, these are some tentative ideas for a Christian economics. I doubt that abstract arguments alone will yield a greater acceptance or a greater place in society for Christian economics. Christian economists will have to show that by introducing their perspective it is possible to gain a better understanding of actual events in the world.

MY CURRENT THINKING

So where am I today? I am no longer much of a believer in the idea of economic progress in a redemptive sense. However, I do think that more food on the table is better than less food and the same thought applies to housing, clothing, medical care, and other material concerns. Economic progress, one might say, is probably a necessary but not a sufficient condition for saving the world—assuming that can happen at all. Thus, I still think it is important to introduce economic considerations into the policy debate. However, I also think that economists should make drastic changes in the ways that they study economic systems and issues. Their economic methods should be much less formally quantitative and much more historical and institutional.

I am still critical of environmental religion, although in some ways I may have become more sympathetic. I find myself in agreement with environmentalists on the exaggerations of a simple belief in the redeeming benefits of economic growth and progress. I also think that environmentalists should be given credit for directing the attention of Americans to environmental problems. The environmental movement created the political impetus to take important new steps to protect the environment. Even though much of environmental policy has been flawed in its conception, Americans are still better off overall for having taken these steps. There have been some desirable environmental trends such as the improved air quality of the United States over the past 30 years.

In terms of my own religion, I have become more agnostic as a whole. Secular religion, whether economic, environmental, or otherwise, seems to me to have been much overrated in the modern age. A commitment to some kind of religion does seem to me to be necessary to a thriving human existence. I am unwilling to see human beings as simply an elaborate collection of molecules or as the mere byproducts of a random evolutionary process.

However, my own religious ideas are a work in progress. Some of my colleagues at the University of Maryland occasionally chide me for being too much the disinterested observer—for enjoying the Olympian perspective and for being reluctant to make a greater personal commitment to a religious bottom line. One response I give is that each person can have his or her own role. Perhaps my faith is that somehow out of the chaos of modern—and now postmodern—pluralism in religious matters there will emerge something of greater religious certainty in the twenty-first century. It may be enough simply to be a small participant in that process.

Chapter 7

The Economic Ethics of Jesus

David P. Gushee

INTRODUCTION

I rarely emphasize my denominational identity when I speak or write. I am by calling a Christian minister with a specialized service as a teacher–scholar in Christian ethics. I am by conviction an orthodox Christian, an irenic evangelical Christian, and a Baptist, probably in that order of loyalty and priority.

But being "Baptist" provides an opportunity to ask several questions relevant to a discussion into the integration of Christianity in economics. Is there a unique emphasis or cluster of themes that characterize Baptist ethics generally? Is there a distinctive Baptist moral witness on economic life?

Actually, these are issues with which ethicists who claim Baptist identity are just now wrestling. In January 2003 a group of Baptist ethicists gathered at the annual meeting of the Society of Christian Ethics to discuss whether there is such a thing as Baptist ethics and what it might look like. It is certainly the case, I think, that there is no well-developed tradition—not a consensus tradition, anyway—of Baptist *economic* ethics.

What it means to be a Baptist, just like what it means to be a Christian, will always be a contested matter. Those of us who are or have been Southern Baptists in recent decades have lived through a particularly public contesting of the meaning of that identity. But in more subtle ways, the shape and contours of Christian or denominational identity are always contested.

Perhaps the Baptist identity and distinctive character are more unsettled now than in previous generations or more unsettled than that of many other ecclesiastical communities, or perhaps not. I cannot speak with authority about the struggles of others. I can say that little can be claimed with certainty about what it means to be Baptist.

But at a normative theological and moral level, I want to stake the claim that being Baptist means focusing on Jesus Christ. Further, focusing on Jesus Christ means not just attending to his atoning death on the cross, but also his entire sojourn among humanity: his incarnation, teachings, and deeds, as well as his suffering, death, and resurrection. Baptist ethics is Jesus-centered. And I want to claim that being Baptist means attempting to enter the story of Jesus, situate one's own life there as best as one can, and follow after him. Therefore Baptist economic ethics must be both Jesus-centered and discipleship-centered.

My mentor and friend Glen Stassen has labored alongside me for six years to complete a book that we are calling *Kingdom Ethics: Following Jesus in Contemporary Context.* In that book, released in 2003 by InterVarsity Press, we offer an approach to Christian ethics that is relentlessly Jesus-centered. In turn, any book that is relentlessly Jesus-centered is going to be relentlessly centered on the kingdom of God, for this was the heart of Jesus' proclamation and the cause for which he gave his life. Thus I stand with Glen Stassen in presenting material from our book, though the particular arrangement of the material in this essay is my responsibility alone.

In sharp contrast to the other writers in this book, my focus is on the broad ethical issues relating to the contemporary economy. In this chapter I offer an inquiry into the economic ethics of Jesus as presented in the Gospels (especially the Sermon on the Mount), situated in light of what we understand to have been his concept of the reign of God, as well as what is now known about economic and political realities in Jesus' own context. My thesis is that Jesus offered concrete kingdom practices that are just as transformative now as when he first offered them, and just as authoritative for anyone who claims allegiance to Jesus Christ. The challenge for Christian economists is to recognize the significance of these ethical principles in everyday life and their relevance in scholarly pursuits.

JESUS AND THE REIGN OF GOD

"Now after John was arrested, Jesus came to Galilee, proclaiming the good news of God, and saying, 'The time is fulfilled, and the kingdom of God has come near; repent, and believe in the good news'" (Mark 1:14–15). Biblical scholar Gordon Fee has written: "The absolutely central theme of Jesus' mission and message was 'the good news of the kingdom of God'" (1992, p. 8). Jesus taught his followers to "strive first for the kingdom" (Matt 6:33). If Christians want to be followers of Christ, they must seek the kingdom.

But what is the kingdom of God? Is it a place? If so, where is it to be found? Is it a time? If so, when was it, when is it, or when will it be? Is it a vision or an ideal? If so, what does this vision include? Is it a state of affairs of some sort? If so, what characterizes it?

Each of these questions implies further questions related to God's activity and human response—and responsibility. If the kingdom of God is a place, what must one do, if anything, to gain admission? If it is a time, is there anything one can do to hasten it (or delay it)? If it is a vision, or ideal, or state of affairs, what role do Christians have in bringing it about?

Let me dispense with the time dimension first. I say "dispense" because Christians tend to get fixated on the "when" question rather than the "what" question when thinking about the kingdom. Clearly, in Jesus' teaching the kingdom is, as Fee says, "both a future event and a present reality" (1992, p. 11). Jesus celebrated the fact that in himself God was initiating the long-promised salvation of the world, beginning with the covenant people Israel. However, it is also true that Jesus pointed to a future time when this salvation would be fully consummated. So the kingdom is a reality that has been initiated but not yet finalized or consummated. Humanity now lives in the time between the two events.

This begun-but-not-completed kingdom is not a place either on earth or in heaven, as many suppose. It cannot be equated with the church, or with heaven itself. Nor is it a vision, as in a utopian dream of a better world. Nor is it some kind of internal human attitude, as in "the kingdom of God is within you," which is actually a mistranslation of Luke 17:21.

Instead, Jesus taught that the kingdom of God is that state of affairs in which God reigns. It is rooted in the most significant fact about the world: the Earth is a place created and sustained by God, yet characterized by the rebellion against God of those creatures intended to be the pinnacle of the Creator's efforts. Thus the fact of the matter is that God reigns and yet does not reign. God is king, and yet his kingship is rejected—certainly in deed, and often in word as well. When people see a bumper sticker that says something like "Jesus is Lord over Louisville" (or Miami, or Waco, or wherever), they are reading a statement that is both true and false at the same time.

The Old Testament is achingly familiar with this seeming contradiction. The sacred writings of the covenant people Israel, especially after the nation's history collapsed in war and exile, are full of grief over the violation of God's reign and yet redolent with the promise of its future consummation. Jesus did not spin the concept of the reign of God out of whole cloth. Instead, Jesus' proclamation of the kingdom of God must be understood, as Biblical scholar W. D. Davies (1962) put it, "in light of the expectations expressed in the Old Testament, and in Judaism, that, at some future date, God would act for the salvation of His people" (p. 167).

For hundreds of years, faithful Jews had nurtured the hope that God would intervene decisively for the salvation of his people, and indeed for the whole earth. In entertaining such hopes, Jews had ample Biblical material to ponder. In *Kingdom Ethics* (2003), Stassen and Gushee argue that it was particularly through the prophet Isaiah that Jesus seems to have drawn most deeply his understanding and proclamation of what the kingdom looked like.

Sixteen passages in Isaiah tell of God reigning in a way that brings about deliverance or salvation (9:1–7; 11:1–16; 24:14–25:12; 26:1–24; 31:1–32:20; 33:1–24; 35:1–10; 40:1–11; 42:1–44:8; 49:1–26; 51:1–52:12; 52:13–53:12; 54:1–17; 56:1–12; 60:1–22; 61:1–62:12.) We believe these passages of God's deliverance describe what the kingdom of God means in Isaiah—the Biblical book to which Jesus most often referred or alluded when he proclaimed the kingdom. So the next logical question is, Do some characteristics of God's reign recur consistently in these passages, some themes that clarify the content of God's kingdom?

Deliverance or salvation occur in all 16 passages; righteousness or justice occur in 15 of the passages; peace in 14; joy in 12; God's presence as spirit or light in 9 (and God's dynamic presence is implied in all 16). These five characteristics of the reign-of-God are remarkably consistent in the deliverance or reign of God passages. We may conclude that these are characteristics of God's delivering action as described in Isaiah. In addition, healing occurs in seven passages. It may be seen as a mark in its own right, or as part of the themes of peace and restoration of outcasts to community, since major infirmities caused people to be treated as outcasts. Return from exile occurs in nine passages. Therefore, these also may be key ingredients in the reign of God as prophesied by Isaiah.

In summary—acknowledging that I am telescoping a much broader discussion offered in Stassen and Gushee (2003) and in the literature—what Isaiah, and thus very likely Jesus, meant by the reign of God can be summarized in this way:

- God will some day act decisively to deliver his people (and the world) from their suffering.
- God's justice will prevail over current injustice.
- God's peace will bring an end to war and violence.
- God's presence will be acutely felt and experienced.
- Healing of the broken and the ill will take place.
- Outcasts and the exiled will be restored to covenant community.
- God's people will respond with great joy to all that God is doing.

It must be made absolutely clear that in Jesus' teaching the kingdom is something that *God* is doing. God initiates the kingdom; in a sense, God performs the kingdom. It is not a human work. Like a mustard tree, it grows from a tiny seed even while Christians sleep (Matt 13:31 and par.).

However, the kingdom is a divine action that human beings are called to participate in. Almost all kingdom teachings emphasize both God's activity and the call to human response and participation. Thus the fact that the kingdom is being initiated by God demands of people some kind of response; either they are on board, or they are not. Either they are part of the advance of the reign of God, or they are part of what hinders it. A fundamental life-decision is thus required: am I, or am I not, a kingdom person? Do I believe this story, and am I willing to live accordingly?

That is why one should ask not only or even mainly about the timing of the kingdom, but about the characteristics, the marks, of the kingdom. The question of timing does not tell what the kingdom is like, what its characteristics are, or what sort of deeds fit it. Jesus said no one knows when the kingdom will come in the full, future sense (Mark 13:32; Matt 24:36); the point, he said, is not to know the timing or (with apologies to LaHaye and Jenkins, 1996) the sequence of events, but instead to be doing the deeds he teaches so Christians are ready for it (Matt 7:21–27; 22:4–15; 24:42–25:13; Mark 13:32–37; Luke 12:35–48). If Christians put attention on when the kingdom will come, and not on what its characteristics are, they neglect the practices that prepare for it. The result is arcane theological debate, or fatalistic speculation, rather than faithful participation. Identifying the kingdom's characteristics is crucial for Christian ethics, for Christian discipleship, for Christian living, and for the response of faith (i.e., faithfulness).

All of Jesus' moral teachings take their proper context in this light. Jesus is the trailblazer for the reign of God. He both shows and teaches kingdom practices. Followers of Jesus—Christians—are those who apprentice in the kingdom practices of Jesus by obeying his teachings. They do so not merely because they want to go to heaven or be decent people but because they really believe in the narrative of the reign of God, really have chosen to make the reign of God the purpose of their lives, and really want the joy of participating in its advance.

Therefore, Christians work for justice and righteousness. They teach and practice the way of peacemaking in relationships. They experience the presence of God and help others do the same. They facilitate healing of bodies and spirits. They restore outcasts and lonely ones to community. They live joyfully in the Spirit of God. And in general, they give their lives to participating in the delivering salvation that God has brought to the earth in Jesus Christ. This kingdom agenda becomes what their lives are about. They live for God by practicing kingdom values.

JESUS' CONFRONTATION WITH ECONOMIC INJUSTICE

In light of this understanding of the kingdom, I propose that Jesus offered two main types of kingdom teachings and practices in the area of economic life. These were, first, direct prophetic confrontations of economic injustice, and second, declarations to his disciples about how to get free from sinful patterns of attitude and behavior related to money, wealth, and possessions. These teachings were inextricably related to each other, and both were grounded in his kingdom vision.

North American churches have tended to evade or misunderstand both dimensions of Jesus' teaching. They have often completely missed his confrontation with economic injustice. And when they have noticed his striking teachings related to money, they have evaded them or spiritualized them to an inelegant death.

Let me begin with Jesus' confrontation with economic injustice. Jesus identified especially strongly with the tradition of the prophets of Israel. This is clear in the Gospels, and it is clear now in much New Testament scholarship. It was not so clear to previous scholarship that was influenced by anti-Semitism, by a liberal preference for "universal truths" rather than the historical particularity of Jesus, and by less attention to the historical context of Israel in Jesus' day. This is being corrected. N. T. Wright (1996) begins his book on the historical Jesus by saying: "Jesus' public persona within first-century Judaism was that of a prophet, and the content of His prophetic proclamation was the 'kingdom' of Israel's God. . . . The prophetic aspect of Jesus' work is often surprisingly ignored" (p. 11). He argues that Jesus' mission also was as Messiah and Savior, but Christians cannot understand his mission accurately if they wrench him out of the tradition of the prophets.

Jesus was proclaiming a message from the covenant God, and living it out with symbolic actions. He was confronting the people with the folly of their ways, summoning them to a different path, and expecting to suffer the consequences of doing so. Elijah had stood alone against the prophets of Baal and against the wickedness of King Ahab. Jeremiah had announced the doom of the temple and the nation, in the face of royalty, priests, and official prophets. All were accused of troubling the status quo. When people "saw" Jesus as a prophet, this was the kind of model they had in mind (Wright, 1996, p. 167f.)

A second development in New Testament scholarship is new attention to Jesus' symbolic attack on the temple system. (For only a few examples, see Myers, 1997, pp. 79–86; p. 126f., p. 300ff., p. 350ff.; Sanders, 1985, chap. 1; Herzog, 2000, chap. 6; Bockmuehl, 1994, chap. 3; Borg, 1998, chap. 7; Wright, 1996, pp. 333–36, pp. 413–28, pp. 490–3.) Scholars are seeing that it was not merely a "cleansing" of the temple, but a prophetic and symbolic attack on the whole temple system for practicing a cover up of injustice—the same kind of attack offered by both Isaiah 56 and Jeremiah 7. These are the two passages that the Gospels report Jesus as quoting when he overturned the tables of the moneychangers and "would not allow anyone to carry anything through the temple" (Mark 11:16, 11:15–17 & par.).

N. T. Wright (1996, p. 335) points out that in six different passages, Jesus prophesied the destruction of the temple. Wright disagrees with the liberal scholar John Dominic Crossan (1996) on much, but here he says that Crossan comes very close to the right answer on what caused Jesus to be crucified: "Crossan thinks, and I fully agree with him, that Jesus' action in the temple was a symbolic destruction; that these words and this action followed with a close logic from the rest of Jesus' agenda" (p. 61).

David Garland (1996) writes that Jesus' action at the temple was neither an act of violent revolution, nor merely a "cleansing" or reform of the temple, but a symbolic prophetic action of protest against injustice and its cover-up. Why would Jesus merely try to cleanse the temple when he predicted it would soon be destroyed? "If sacrificial animals cannot be purchased, then sacrifice must end. If no vessel can be carried through the temple, then all cultic activity must cease." And if money cannot be made, then the financial support for the temple and the priests will be gone. "Jesus does not seek to purify current temple worship but symbolically attacks the very function of the temple and heralds its destruction" (Garland, 1996, p. 433–39). His hostility to the temple emerges as a charge at his trial (Mark 14:58) and as a taunt at the cross (Mark 15:29).

Jesus cited two passages from the prophets as he carried out this prophetic action. Isaiah 56:7, "My house shall be called a house of prayer for all peoples," is part of the declaration in Isaiah 56:1–8 that God's purpose is to bless all who are being excluded, including foreigners, eunuchs, and outcasts. "During His entire ministry Jesus has been gathering in the impure outcasts and the physically maimed, and has even reached out to Gentiles. He expects the temple to embody this inclusive love. . . . In Jesus' day the temple had become a nationalistic symbol that served only to divide Israel from the nations" (Garland, 1996, p. 438). And the court where God intended the Gentiles to worship had been taken over as a trading post.

Jeremiah 7 says God's people should not keep claiming they have the temple of the Lord, when they need to amend their ways and truly execute justice with each other, not to oppress the alien, the orphan, or the widow, or shed innocent blood and go after other gods. The temple is functioning as a cover-up for injustice, what Bonhoeffer (1995) called "cheap grace." If God's people continue to practice injustice while claiming God is on their side, because they have the temple (or the church), God will destroy the temple (or the church) and cast them out of God's sight. By quoting from Jeremiah 7, Jesus

> denounces the false security that the sacrificial cult breeds. . . . The den is the place where robbers retreat after having committed their crimes. It is their hideout, a place of security and refuge. Calling the temple a robbers' den is therefore not a cry of outrage against any dishonest business practices in the temple. Jesus indirectly attacks them for allowing the temple to degenerate into a safe hiding place where people think that they find forgiveness and fellowship with God no matter how they act on the outside. Jesus' prophetic action and words attack a false trust in the efficacy of the temple sacrificial system. The leaders of the people think that they can rob widows' houses (Mark 12:40) and then perform the prescribed sacrifices according to the prescribed patterns at the prescribed times in the prescribed purity in the prescribed sacred space and then be safe and secure from all alarms. They are wrong. (Garland, 1996, p. 439)

Jesus came proclaiming the reign of God. The reign of God in Isaiah announced God's justice as deliverance of the outcasts, the poor, and the oppressed from the domination of greed and concentrated power, and the restoration of community with peace. It called for repentance for injustice. Would it not be strange if Jesus announced the kingdom but avoided these central themes of God's justice and repentance for injustice?

One can hear persons who, influenced by the secularizing two-realm split between private and public, say Jesus taught only love for individuals and not justice in relation to political and economic powers and authorities. Perhaps they think Rome was the government and the high priests were only religious. Perhaps they forget that state, church, and economic wealth were not separated but very much mixed together on the same hill and in the same temple in Jerusalem, and that Rome allowed the Jewish authorities to do most of the daily ruling. When Jesus confronted the representatives of the temple authority, he was confronting the public authorities of his time.

Markus Bockmuehl (1994) offers a very important point related to the social, economic, and political context in which Jesus operated. He points out that Jesus

> was put to death by the Romans following a plot among the aristocracy. . . . The priestly aristocracy of Jerusalem with their private police gangs worked closely together with the Roman authorities to crack down at any hint of insurrection. . . . The corruption of the priestly aristocracy in Jerusalem invited comparison with the earlier prophetic oracles of judgment and destruction. . . . Of the 28 high priests between 37 BC and AD 70, all but two came from four power-hungry, illegitimate non-Zadokite families. . . . Recent historical study is making increasingly clear that the operation of the Temple . . . was in the hands of a vast economic and religious power network. . . . Traders had only very recently moved into the Court of the Gentiles at the invitation of Caiaphas. . . . The Mishnah gives evidence of hugely inflated price fixing for sacrificial doves, which were the offering of the poor. . . . The hierarchy operated agents and hit squads known as "men of violence" and the "big men of the priesthood." . . . During those two decades [of Jesus' teenage years and adulthood] Annas and Caiaphas together enjoyed unrivalled power as a result of successful collaboration with the occupation forces of Rome. . . . Josephus and the rabbinic writings also concur in offering some most remarkable descriptions of the utter luxury and extravagance of the priestly aristocracy in Jerusalem . . . (pp. 69–71)

Furthermore, the 90 percent of the population who were peasant farmers and village craftsmen like those in Galilee produced most of the wealth. But the 10 percent of the people who were the economic and religio-political aristocracy in the cities, and their supporters, siphoned off over half of the products by taxes, required tithes, and charges for sacrifices and temple services. The priestly authorities, Sadducees, and also the Pharisees developed teachings and religious traditions that gave authority to this centralization of economic power. The hierarchy was in collusion with the wealthy, and with the Roman empire. (Among other critics, Borg, 1998, pp. x, 7, 12–14, 20ff., 33, et passim; Sanders,

1985, p. 309ff.; Herzog, 2000, pp. 91f., 94f., 102–4, 127, 137, 150, 171f., 191, 219, 233–35, 241–44, question the extent of this burden.)

Did Jesus teach only individual love or did he carry out prophetic action and teach justice that challenged and undermined the authority of this aristocracy? In Isaiah, justice is not merely an ideal for good individuals in their private life, but is a righteous demand that has the strength to confront those who have power. That is one absolutely essential contribution of justice in a sinful world where concentration of power needs restraint, checks and balances, and limits on greed. God's will for people cannot be fulfilled without justice.

One can count thirty-nine times in the Synoptic Gospels, plus parallels, when Jesus confronted the powers and authorities of his day. In addition, Jesus performed practices and gave other teachings that, even if not explicitly stated as confrontation of authorities, surely did challenge the theological ideology of those in power. Four themes run through Jesus' confrontations over injustice, indicating four dimensions of the justice that Jesus stood for as the will of God. They are strikingly close to themes discovered in the kingdom of God passages in Isaiah. Jesus attacked

1. The injustice of greed, and called for and enacted justice for the poor and hungry.
2. The injustice of domination, and called for and enacted power as mutual servanthood.
3. The injustice of violence, and called for and enacted peacemaking.
4. The injustice of exclusion from community, and called for and enacted inclusion of outcasts.

All four themes are important. For my purposes, working with the first can cement the claim that Jesus offered prophetic indictments of economic injustice.

Deliverance from extortion of the poor by the powerful, and deeds of deliverance of the poor from their need were central to the preaching of John the Baptist. John declared, "'Whoever has two coats must share with anyone who has none; and whoever has food must do likewise'" (Luke 3:11). He told the tax collectors, "'Collect no more than the amount prescribed for you'" (Luke 3:13). He told the soldiers, "'Do not extort money from anyone by threats or false accusation'" (Luke 3:14). Jesus praised John the Baptist as God's prophet and said, by contrast, "'Those who put on fine clothing and live in luxury are in royal palaces'" (Luke 7:25). He also confronted Zacchaeus for his extortion as a tax collector, and Zacchaeus not only repented but declared he would restore what was just to those he extorted (Luke 19:1–10).

The parable of the unforgiving slave (Matt 18:23–35) is surely a confrontation of persons who do not forgive debts. On the one hand, it concerns forgiveness from the heart of one's fellow human (18:35). But it is also about large debts of money that the poor owe to their creditors. The word for debt (18:27) ordinarily means a loan of money, and release is the word Josephus uses to refer to the Jubilee, when he says all "debtors are freed from their debts" (Hultgren, 2002, p. 26). The parable portrays the experience of many poor people in Jesus' time, too deep in debt to pay back their loans. Thus the parable is also a confrontation of unforgiving creditors who do not forgive debts, and it fits the theme of Jubilee that Andre Trocme (1973) and John Howard Yoder (1994, chap. 3) have brought to our attention.

Luke 16:14–15 introduces Jesus' saying by explaining, "The Pharisees, who were lovers of money, heard all this, and they ridiculed him. So he said to them, 'You are those who justify [dikaiountes] yourselves in the sight of others, but God knows your hearts.'" In Matthew 23:16–19, 25, Jesus pointed to the scribes and Pharisees' fixation on gold and offerings, by which they forced undue hardship on those who could not offer such expensive gifts. Jesus said, "'You clean the outside of the cup and of the plate, but inside they are full of greed and self-indulgence'" (Matt 23:25). In Mark 12:38–44, Jesus identified the same pattern of injustice when he warned against the scribes who "devour widows' houses" while maintaining a façade of piety with their long prayers. The temple, which was supposed to support widows and orphans, had been turned into "the institution that extracts their last copper coins" (Herzog, 2000, p. 189). In Matthew 15:3–9 and Mark 7:9–13, Jesus said to the Pharisees, "Why do you break the commandment of God for the sake of your tradition? For God said, 'Honor your father and your mother' . . . But you say that . . . that person need not honor the father" (Matt 15:4–5). A few verses later, Jesus quoted Isaiah 29:13, confirming the theme of his connection with Isaiah. Similarly, in Matthew 12:1–8, Mark 2:23–28, and Luke 6:1–5, Jesus defended feeding the hungry on the Sabbath, saying to the Pharisees, "If you had known what this means, 'I desire mercy and not sacrifice,' you would not have condemned the guiltless" (Matt 12:7), quoting Hosea 6:6. Acts of mercy to the hungry are acts of covenant justice in the Old Testament. As we noted above, Jesus' symbolic attack on the temple quoted Jeremiah 7:5f., which calls for truly acting justly to the alien, the orphan, and the widow.

Jesus' teaching, "Give to the emperor the things that are the emperor's, and to God the things that are God's" (Mark 12:17; see also Matt 22:15–22; Luke 20:20–26), concerns paying tribute tax to Caesar. Ched Myers (1997, p. 310) says the question was "a test of loyalty that divided collaborators from subversives against the backdrop of revolt." The tax was oppressive to the poor, and it was idolatrous for the faithful Jews. Jesus was so loyal to justice to the poor, and he so emphatically taught service to God alone, that his action of getting the Pharisees and Herodians to come up with a coin, and then holding it up and asking whose image was on it, exposed their collaboration with the Roman power structure and distanced himself from it. He was confronting the injustice of the Roman tax and the collaboration of the Pharisees and Herodians, while at the same time advocating peaceful conduct. Jesus' reply is an antithetical parallelism, in which the second line, "Render to God what is God's" actually includes everything since everything belongs to God. It means "Render to Caesar only what is consistent with God's will." In sum, Jesus fulfilled the words Isaiah spoke concerning God: "For you have been a refuge to the poor, a refuge to the needy in their distress" (Isa 25:4).

Jesus fulfilled the theme of deliverance of the poor and needy from the greed of the powerful, which is a key mark of God's deliverance in Isaiah. The first chapter of Isaiah begins with judgment on the injustice that flows from greed:

> Your princes are rebels
> and companions of thieves.
> Every one loves a bribe
> and runs after gifts.
> They do not defend the orphan,
> and the widow's cause does not
> come before them. (Isa 1:23)

This is God's word. Jesus taught that God cared deeply for the poor and the powerless. He not only taught it; he enacted it. Jesus fed the poor and hungry, and taught the disciples the practice of sharing with those in need. He brought the way of deliverance. The kingdom began in Jesus.

"YOU CANNOT SERVE GOD AND WEALTH": MAMMON AND THE SERMON

So Jesus offered stark prophetic indictments of economic injustice, hurling his charges against the very centers of religious and political power of his time, earning their enduring outrage, which culminated in his execution. But that was not the extent of his teaching about such matters. Jesus offered a different way of life altogether when he addressed his disciples about the economic dimension of their lives, such as in the Sermon on the Mount (Matt 5:1–7:29). It was the way of the kingdom; it is the way of the kingdom. Those who want to participate in the kingdom's advance must renounce the way that Jesus condemned and take a new path. His teachings tell of what the path consists. This interpretation of the significance of Jesus' teachings hinges on a pivotal discovery that Glen Stassen first made some years ago, and that is now gaining adherents in the Biblical studies community (Stassen & Gushee, 2003). I must pause and offer a brief methodological excursus.

Over long centuries, a tradition developed in the church that tended to compartmentalize and marginalize Jesus with one kind of dualism or another. A key step in that accommodation was and is to teach that the Sermon on the Mount in particular, and Jesus' teachings in general, consist of hard teachings, ideals too high for humans to reach; lovely sentiments but impossible for practical living. Once that step is taken, it is easier to argue that people need some other ethic that they can practice—which almost always turns out to be an ethic that accepts the authority of some secular power or simply offers a collective shrug that surrenders to "how things are."

In terms of the Sermon, it has been taught that Jesus offers antitheses, in which he prohibits anger, lust, divorce, money, oaths, resistance to evil, and commands that his followers renounce all rights. Then people realize that they cannot do these things. So they say these are hard teachings, high ideals, and very strenuous demands. They praise them for being so idealistic and then conclude they cannot follow them in practice and must adopt another ethic that comes from somewhere else. They compartmentalize Jesus' teachings as meant for attitudes but not actions, or for repentance but not obedience, or for another future dispensation but not the present time, or merely as illustrations of general principles like love but not meant to be followed in particular.

We instead claim that the pattern of the Sermon is not twofold antitheses, but threefold transforming initiatives. And that therefore, the emphasis in interpretation is to be placed not on an alleged idealistic prohibition, but on the realistic way of deliverance in the transforming initiatives. First, Jesus offers some statement from the Hebrew Bible or traditional Jewish understandings of the content of righteousness. Then he offers a diagnosis of vicious cycles or patterns of bondage that keep people from obeying God's will as revealed or declared by this traditional statement. In the climactic section of each saying, he proposes a transforming initiative that can break the grip of sin and lead to practices that obey God's will. Sometimes he follows up with an explanation to clarify the content or rationale of his teaching.

Throughout the Sermon, the emphasis in Jesus' teaching is the transforming initiatives, where the imperative verbs are positioned. These initiatives are regular practices that are commanded by Jesus for Christians to take, practices that participate in God's way of gracious deliverance from the vicious cycles that people get stuck in. Jesus teaches practice norms. They are not mere inner attitudes, or vague intentions, or moral convictions only, but regular practices to be engaged in. As people engage in them, they learn better and better ways to do God's will.

That is what Jesus is doing, then, in his economic teachings as in other areas. In pursuit of the reign of God, he is diagnosing the vicious cycles people get into and offering transformative practices that can get them free of sin and in new patterns that participate in the kingdom's advance. Let me try this model out on two sections (or triads) within the Sermon on the Mount: Matthew 6:19–23 and 6:24–34.

All scholars agree that 6:19 begins a new unit. It begins with a traditional or proverbial teaching, a negative imperative resembling the traditional negative teachings of Matthew 5:21ff. Literally translated, it reads: "Do not treasure up for yourselves treasures on earth." The play on words, "treasure up treasures," connotes hoarding for show, greed, and stinginess.

The vicious cycle is then clear: "where moth and rust consume and where thieves break in and steal" (6:19; cf. Jas 5:1–6). Material possessions have always been susceptible to decay and theft, but Jesus' first-century listeners would have been acutely aware of the problem. Thieves could dig right through the walls of most homes and steal any strongbox in which precious possessions might be stored. Some dealt with this problem by hiding valuables in caves or burying them in the ground, but both clothing and coins could easily be ruined in such hiding places (Keener, 1993, p. 63). The folly of accumulating excess goods in such circumstances is obvious. And yet many devoted their lives to it in Jesus' time, as many do in our own. It is one of humanity's besetting, and most pitiable, vices.

The transforming initiative is found in the imperative in verse 20: "But treasure up for yourselves treasures in heaven." This text is quite similar to a saying found in the apocryphal book of Tobit: "If you have many possessions, make your gift from them in proportion; if few, do not be afraid to give according to the little you have. So you will be laying up a good treasure for yourself against the day of necessity" (Tob 4:8–9). The concept of treasures in heaven as opposed to treasures on earth is also mentioned elsewhere in Jesus' teaching (Matt 19:21; Mark 10:21; Luke 18:22; Matt 13:44; Luke 12:33) and in the epistles (1 Tim 6:19; Jas 5:3). The idea is that a life of economic generosity trades earthly treasures for divine approval in this life and the next, an exchange of "treasures" well worth making.

This first explanation is linked to two others: "where your treasure is, there your heart will be also" (Matt 6:21), and "if your eye is healthy, your whole body will be full of light" (Matt 6:22). These comments make a fine illustration of the claim that Jesus did not teach impossible ideals, but transforming initiatives that participate in the deliverance of the kingdom.

"Heaven," for Matthew, is "the sphere of God's rule where His will is done . . . To have one's treasure in heaven means to submit oneself totally to that which is in heaven—God's sovereign rule" (Guelich, 1982, pp. 327–28). The contrast Jesus is drawing is not between this life and the life after, but between this life characterized by profound, misery-causing injustice, and God's inbreaking reign characterized by salvation, justice, peace, and joy in God's presence. The transforming initiative is to invest one's treasures in God's reign of justice and love through practices of economic generosity and justice-making.

This teaching does not idealistically reject personal property or the holding of any possessions as has sometimes been argued, but instead rejects "treasuring up treasures"—stinginess, greed, hoarding, lack of generosity. The reference to vision is critical here. The ability to "see" the coming eschatological era and to respond with appropriate deeds constitutes "messianic salvation" (Gundry, 1994, p. 113). As well, the "evil" eye in Jewish teaching connotes stinginess and greed, while the "healthy" or single eye connotes generosity. Matthew 6:22–23 pulls these two themes together and could perhaps be restated something like this: "If in view of the coming eschaton you see your neighbor's need rightly and respond generously, your entire self blazes with the light of God's presence; but if you close your eyes to your neighbor's need, your self is full of the darkness of God's absence, and that darkness is very great indeed." That then leads back to Matthew 6:21: Either path you choose reveals the true condition of your heart.

A genuinely impossible ideal would be to do what so many, including Christians, in wealthy cultures do: practice piling up wealth and extravagant possessions while at the same time claiming to give as generously to the needy as they "can"; and, for that matter, to live extravagantly while at the same time not being affected by such spending choices in their "hearts." Jesus' teaching is far more realistic: invest your possessions generously in God's reign of justice and mercy, and you will find your heart invested there as well.

Sondra Wheeler (1995, p. 68) nicely points out that a transformed economic praxis such as Jesus teaches here "*follows* from faith, the reasonable response of one who perceives in Jesus the advent of the kingdom." In other words, disciples do not live simply and give generously in order to be counted worthy of being disciples. Instead, because they are disciples of Jesus and are invested in his eschatological project it naturally follows that they reorient their lives in every area, including economic life. This claim fits with the theme that kingdom ethics is grace-based, rooted in an invitation to participate in the inbreaking of God's reign through Jesus Christ. Disciples are those who believe the story of Jesus the Messiah, enter it, and live accordingly.

Matthew 6:24 reads: "No one can [is able to] serve two masters; for a slave will either hate the one and love the other, or be devoted to the one and despise the other." This statement takes the form of a traditional Jewish wisdom proverb (Guelich, 1982, p. 333; Davies & Allison, 1988, p. 642; Betz, 1995, p. 456). Hillel is reported as saying, "the more possessions, the more care" (Hagner, 1993, p. 159). The idea that one cannot serve God and money "was far-flung in antiquity" (Allison, 1989, p. 145). As expected in the traditional teaching part of a Matthean triad, it is negative, and it is not an imperative.

The vicious cycle is named directly in Matthew 6:24c: "You cannot [literally: are not able to] serve God and wealth [mammon]." Those who attempt to do so are like those slaves who attempt to serve two imperious masters—they are placed in an impossible position. Only one master can be served. The effort to evade this fact of existence is simply a futile self-deception. Matthew 6:25–33 then offers four exhortations: "do not worry (25) . . . look at the birds (26) . . . consider the lilies (28) . . . strive first for the kingdom" (33).

The thrust of the transforming initiative is found in the latter three imperatives, climaxing in the famous exhortation to "strive first for the kingdom of God and His righteousness." These imperatives teach people to give themselves over to trusting participation in the dynamic, gracious, delivering presence of God. In looking at the provision God majestically offers for the flora and fauna, they are called away from anxiety to trust in God the Creator-Sustainer-Redeemer. When people make the critical life decision to devote "eyes"and "heart"—themselves—to participation in the reign of God, they break loose from the vicious cycle of "mammonism" and are set free to live for justice with singleness of purpose. Not only does this decision produce useful instruments of kingdom work, it is both wise and reasonable as well. As Jesus reminds in his explanation, worry never added a day to life or clothed and fed anybody. "Today's trouble is enough for today" (Matt 6:34). Trust God for "daily bread" and devote oneself to the kingdom.

The thematic consistency of this entire passage (Matt 6:19–34) is summarized nicely by Guelich (1982):

> Since God's sovereign rule and all the benefits for our material needs come from God to us, this passage suggests by implication that we can become a part of God's redemptive force in history by sharing these benefits with those who are in need. . . . Part of the presence of the Kingdom is indeed material blessings. Therefore, we can hardly live under God's reign, receive His blessings, and not use them to help alleviate the evil of hunger and need elsewhere. . . . Not only do we recognize that all we have comes from God, but we also recognize that sharing that with others to remove their suffering is to defeat the enemy and to "seek the Kingdom . . . on earth as in heaven." (373)

It turns out to be quite important to read the exhortation against worry in light of the emphasis on economic generosity and the economic justice that characterizes God's reign ("strive first for the kingdom of God and His *dikaiosyne* [righteousness/justice].") Seeing this can help people avoid reducing Jesus' moral teaching on economic life to something like the following understanding, so common in the churches: "enjoy your material comforts and try not to worry too much if you don't have everything you want."

Instead, in a context characterized by extraordinary economic exploitation in Jesus' own day and long economic depression in Matthew's time, Jesus is teaching about the kind of compassionate and merciful justice that delivers the poor from poverty and restores them into community. This is a justice teaching, not merely a psychological teaching. And it is a discipleship teaching, a summons to serve God's compassionate reign through acts of justice-advancing compassion toward the most economically vulnerable and oppressed.

Let me pull together what I have said about Jesus' teaching. Compare my approach with the way that Jesus' economic teaching is normally interpreted:

Jesus' Teaching	*"Realistic" Objection*	*Sifted Norm*
Do not be concerned about money or property, God will provide.	People cannot really count on God providing for their needs, however much they might wish they could.	Therefore, Jesus offered an ideal which people should strive for, an attitude they should adopt as they pursue customary economic practices in society.

Traditional Righteousness	*Vicious Cycle*	*Transforming Initiative*
Matthew 6:19a Do not store up for yourselves treasures on earth.	Matthew 6:19b Moth and rust destroy, thieves break in and steal.	Matthew 6:20 Store up for yourselves treasures in heaven.
Matthew 6:24a No one can serve two masters.	Matthew 6:24b Divided loyalties: attempting to serve God wholeheartedly while worrying about wealth and what it can buy.	Matthew 6:25–34 Seek first God's kingdom and justice, trusting that God will provide for basic needs.

In short, working only with the Sermon on the Mount to this point, certain essentials of a Jesus-centered economic ethic emerge. Seeing the inbreaking reign of God when most do not, the follower of Jesus is overjoyed at the opportunity to participate in the kingdom's dynamic advance in every area, economic life included. Living simply, not hoarding wealth, and trusting God to meet basic material needs are practices that free people to offer generosity to and seek justice for and with the poor and hungry and, in general, to follow Jesus. Finally, in turning hearts and eyes in this direction they themselves enjoy the added benefit of a remarkable personal liberation that yanks them free from greed, acquisitiveness, and a fruitless worry over treasures that will all too soon pass away.

JESUS AND MONEY ELSEWHERE IN THE GOSPELS

Even outside the Sermon on the Mount, the Gospels offer an abundance of testimony concerning Jesus' teaching about money, wealth, poverty, and greed. Let me close with a brief recounting of five of these key themes. All Christians should consider applications to personal life, and the life of communities of faith.

Possessions Are Intrinsically Insignificant Beyond the Basic Sufficiency Provided by Our Gracious God

In the Sermon on the Mount, Jesus called his listeners to trust God rather than worry about food, drink, and clothing. To many interpreters, this has seemed a "hard saying" or "counsel of perfection." It does not seem like such an impossible ideal, however, when one considers Jesus' emphasis on the relative insignificance of possessions.

Luke 12:13ff. tells the story of the man asking Jesus to settle an inheritance dispute the man is having with his brother. Jesus refuses to get involved in estate arbitration (12:14), and moves on to warn his listeners: "Take care! Be on your guard against all kinds of greed; for one's life does not consist in the abundance of possessions."

It must be emphasized clearly that having a basic sufficiency of food and drink, clothing, shelter, and medical care is *not* insignificant. Jesus affirms the need to feed, clothe, and house the human body both by his teachings (cf. Matt 25:31ff.) and his actions of feeding and healing. Jesus must not be interpreted as a gnostic or dualistic dreamer who cared nothing for the human body and its needs. Money and possessions have value as a resource and especially for helping others in need (Wheeler, 1995, pp. 132–33).

The spiritual–moral problem develops, of course, when people ascribe undue significance to possessions. It is easy for modern people to think of this as a uniquely contemporary problem in light of the deluge of skillful advertising one experiences that tells a series of lies about the great significance of this or that food, television, gadget, or car. But the fact that Jesus addressed the issue shows that finding one's life in the abundance of possessions is a human problem rather than a modern problem alone. The issue has to do with treating possessions, as Joel Green (1997) puts it, "as an alternative landmark according to which one might define one's life, and thus as a peril to eternal life" (p. 489, n. 34).

Misreading the Value of Possessions Stimulates Greed

It is no coincidence that Jesus employed images related to sight when speaking of the problem of treasuring up treasures on earth. For in a sense this is fundamentally a problem of vision—that is, moral perception. Misperceiving the value of possessions leads one to moral decisions characterized by greed, which can be defined as an excessive and inordinate desire or even love for money (cf. 1 Tim 6:9–10) and the things money can buy.

We have already seen in Matthew 6:24 the intrinsic contrast between love of God and love of wealth, with Jesus saying that one cannot manage to do both. Greed is a spiritual–moral disorder, according to Jesus' teaching. Rooted in a fundamental misunderstanding of the relative value of possessions and of the role that possessions can actually play in a person's life, greed misleads men and women into ascribing inordinate value to that which is not worthy of it. When wealth, or the possessions wealth can buy, ascends into a position of inordinate value, even love, it is both a form of idolatry and a pitiful delusion contrary to the true best interests of the human being. Seeing wealth as an occasion for idolatry is a major Old Testament theme, especially in the prophets, and Jesus (as well as other New Testament writers) picks up and develops this theme (Wheeler, 1995, pp. 123–24, 129).

The delusional nature of greed is illustrated in a terrifying way by the parable of the rich fool (Luke 12:16–21). Here a wealthy farmer and landowner is blessed with an especially abundant harvest. Unwilling to sell the excess produce on a saturated market, unable to find a place to store all this grain, and, apparently, his many other "goods" (12:18), he embarks on the ambitious project of tearing down all his barns to build larger ones. That very night, he gets a rude surprise: "'You fool! This very night your life is being demanded of you. And the things you have prepared, whose will they be?' So it is with those who store up treasures for themselves but are not rich toward God" (12:20–21). To live in greed or love possessions is to stake one's life on the transitory and vain, to reject God and God's will, and thus to invite divine judgment.

Greed Encourages a Lifestyle of Luxury, Pride, Hoarding, Self-indulgence, Oppression, and Lack of Generosity

Something else is illustrated by this story. The problem with greed is not just that it is a personal spiritual disorder, but that it leads to sins against one's neighbor, in particular hoarding and lack of generosity. This theme links the others I have been exploring in this essay: Jesus' prophetic critique of economic injustice and his transformative teachings to his disciples. The link is that the greed that causes economic injustice ultimately has the most profound roots in moral and spiritual perception and misvaluing. The clear implication of the story of the rich fool is that he should have responded to God's overabundant provision by sharing with those less fortunate. Some might have been able to eat who otherwise would not. This would have stored up treasures in heaven; instead the landowner chose treasures on earth, only to have them rudely snatched away. His greed blinded him to the obvious moral responsibility to aid his neighbor.

We have already seen that Jesus taught in continuity with both Old Testament and rabbinic Judaism in enjoining extensive almsgiving and economic generosity. The person whose heart is given over to God gives to her neighbor with openheartedness, in so doing offering devotion to God. This is part of what is going on in the story of the widow's mite (Mark 12:41; Luke 21:1–4), in which the desperately poor widow is commended for her sacrificial generosity. The pivotal account of the great judgment in Matthew 25:31ff. makes entrance into eternal life contingent upon feeding the hungry, welcoming the stranger, clothing the naked, and visiting the sick and imprisoned. Here we see that generosity encompasses both giving material goods and service to those in need.

This dynamic surely is central to Jesus' intention when he calls followers to sell their possessions. In Luke 12:33, a passage that largely parallels Matthew 6:24–34 in the Sermon on the Mount, Jesus is reported to have also said: "Sell your possessions, and give alms." Luke 14:33 reads, "None of you can become my disciple if you do not give up all your possessions."

The most familiar of these passages is surely the story of the rich man (often called the rich young ruler recorded in Matt 19:16–30, Mark 10:17–31, and Luke 18:18–30). Here Jesus encounters what appears to be an earnest seeker. He is honest in his search to find out "what must I do to inherit eternal life?" (Mark 10:17). Christians often dismiss the man's answer when he claims to have kept the moral teachings of the Decalogue since youth, as Jesus suggests (in good Jewish fashion) is required of him. But Jesus never challenges him on this point, instead saying: "You lack one thing; go, sell what you own, and give the money to the poor, and you will have treasure in heaven; then come, follow me" (10:21). The man is shocked by this demand and goes away "grieving, for he had many possessions" (10:22). Jesus goes on to warn his disciples about the dangers of wealth and to say "it is easier for a camel to go through the eye of a needle than for someone who is rich to enter the kingdom of God" (10:25).

This teaching is so often evaded. The man is described as having the wrong priorities or having a wrong attitude toward money. True enough, perhaps, but evasive of the central point: the man's attachment to his possessions both manifests an inordinate love for them, which blocks generosity to the poor, and leads him to say no to following Jesus. Jesus really did ask the man to sell all that he had, to give it all to the poor, and to embark on a new life of itinerant kingdom poverty with the community of disciples. Those who followed Jesus frequently did exactly this, selling their possessions, giving the money to the poor or contributing it to the common purse that supported Jesus' movement and ensured that all had their basic needs met (cf. 1 John 3:17–18; Acts 4:32–37, 5:1–11; 2 Cor 8:13–15; Garland, 1996, pp. 396f.; Hays, 1996, p. 464). And Jesus really did say that wealth posed a mortal spiritual threat. No exegetical gymnastics related to an imagined "Needle's Eye" gate in Jerusalem (a fabrication first suggested in the 11th century!) can counteract the obvious import of the text (Garland, 1996, p. 401).

We would be better off taking Jesus at his word, and believing that wealth—however acquired, by work or by inheritance, by luck or by labor—presents profound spiritual dangers. This does not mean that no person of wealth can enter into eternal life; Jesus himself did not make this claim. It does mean that the person who finds himself in a position of considerable wealth should take careful heed of the state of his soul as evidenced by his practices.

This is also the significance of the unforgettable story of Lazarus and the rich man in Luke 16:19–31. Here a stark contrast is drawn between the rich man—not given a name, in an ironic reversal of social realities (Green, 1997, p. 606)—and the poor beggar named Lazarus. The rich man has a superfluity of the most luxurious clothing and sumptuous food and drink (16:19). Poor Lazarus has nothing. He has been tossed outside the gates of the rich man and is given nary a scrap. At death, their conditions of suffering and privilege are reversed, with no explicit explanation—the rich man is in torment, Lazarus in Abraham's bosom. It is hard to avoid the conclusion (not that many have not attempted it) that it was the inebriated unconcern of the rich man for his obviously suffering neighbor that led to his eternal downfall. In his luxury and greed he had abandoned the most basic obligations of generosity.

The Deceptive Allure of Wealth Can Choke Discipleship and Imperil the Soul

Clearly, all of the foregoing point to this conclusion. But in one famous passage not yet discussed Jesus makes the point quite clearly. In the parable of the sower and the seed (Mark 4:3–20; Matt 13:3–23; Luke 8:4–15), Jesus outlines four kinds of responses to the "word of the kingdom" (Matt 13:19). These four categories are well-known. What is germane for my purpose is the third type of soil–response, the "thorny." Both Matthew 13:22 and Mark 4:19 say that the seed sown among thorns represents the person whose growth is "choke[d]" by, among other things, *apate tou ploutou* (NRSV–"the lure of wealth," better translated with the NIV as "the deceitfulness of wealth"). Jesus is saying that there is a type of listener to the kingdom's joyful news who begins to respond and to grow in understanding and discipleship but whose progress is choked off by worldly concerns and the deceitfulness of wealth and possessions. Deceitfulness is precisely the right term, for deception involves misrepresenting reality—concealing or distorting the truth about something for the purpose of misleading. Wealth has a kind of power of deceit; it can fool people into seeing in it a kind of earthly salvation ("life") that simply cannot be found there. A marvelous line from the Tennessee Williams classic *Cat on a Hot Tin Roof* captures this nicely:

> The human animal is a beast that eventually has to die. And if he's got money he buys and he buys and he buys. And the reason why he buys everything he can is because of the crazy hope that one of the things he buys will be life everlasting—which it can never be.

All that I have reviewed thus far reminds of why Jesus warns about wealth: the temptation to misread the value of possessions; the consequent greedy spirit; a way of life characterized by luxury, self-indulgence, and lack of generosity; the threat of wealth choking off growth in discipleship—all of these are clear teachings of Jesus that also find confirmation in everyday life if people look with discernment on the world around them.

Jesus Identifies with the Poor and Promises Abundance and Justice in a Coming "Great Reversal"

Perhaps it is not surprising, in view of all of the foregoing, that Jesus—while the bearer of a message for any person in any context—clearly identifies with the poor and hungry, directs his attention to the needs of the poor, celebrates the receptivity of the poor to God, and (in Luke, especially) promises the poor a coming time of abundance and justice that contrasts with their current state of need and oppression. I have shown that the Old Testament hope of the kingdom of God included a vision of justice, of which economic justice for the poor and hungry was an inextricable part. In inaugurating his ministry (Luke 4:18ff.), Jesus appropriates Isaiah 61 and its messianic promise of "good news for the poor," release for the captives, and freedom for the oppressed (cf. Matt 11:5).

Jesus ministered among the poor throughout his brief sojourn here on earth, feeding them, healing them, and addressing systemic injustice that kept them in their wretched condition (see Luke 17). His parables frequently involved the inclusion of the previously excluded poor (cf. Luke 14:15ff.). He enjoined almsgiving for the poor, as we have seen. Zacchaeus the tax collector sought to show his good faith to Jesus by giving his ill-gotten gains to the poor (Luke 19:8). Jesus' disciples and his band of itinerants practiced almsgiving when they had means (cf. Mark 14:5–9 & par.; John 13:29). Jesus attacked and sometimes poked fun at the luxurious (cf. Luke 7:25, 19:16–31) and contrasted their superfluous possessions with the meager lot of the poor.

In Luke, Jesus promises a future time of abundance for the poor, in which they inherit the kingdom of God (Luke 6:20) and finally eat to their fill (6:21), while those currently rich find themselves, at last, on the outside looking in. The same theme takes parabolic form in the story of the rich man and Lazarus. This has been called "the great reversal" (Verhey, 1993; cf. Kraybill, 1978), and it is one of the most radical dimensions of Jesus' teaching, and not just on economic issues (cf. Luke 1:46–55; 14:7–24; 18:9–14, 22–24). It stands in continuity with the prophetic promise of abundance and prosperity for all in the time of God's reign, a joyful contrast with the perennial misery and injustice of poverty in the midst of plenty.

CONCLUSION

Christians living in the wealthiest and most powerful nation in the world, the powerhouse of global capitalism, are daily subjected to the most sophisticated enticements ever devised—enticements not just to buy certain products but to *buy into* a certain way of looking at and living life. It is a way of life that ascribes inordinate value to the acquisition of material goods and indeed thrives on the creation of new "needs" and businesses' cutthroat competition to fulfill those needs. If Christian ethics is following Jesus, it must involve a clear-eyed analysis and finally repudiation of an economic ethos that ratifies the deceitfulness of wealth and makes Mammon the national idol.

This is no mere theoretical preference. I think of lives ruined by this ethos: those who deteriorate into essentially soulless creatures pursuing the latest goodies with zombie-like intensity, going deep into debt to pay for what they do not need; those who have no access to adequate work and no way to provide for their families; those around the world who live in squalor and misery; those whose lives could be turned around by a small commitment on the part of unhappily prosperous people who will never pause from their quest for the latest redemptive gadget to consider the needs of the least of these. This is a condition that has been called "affluenza," and according to Jesus, it is terminal. Even today, Jesus beckons us instead to seek first his kingdom and its justice, for our own redemption and the redemption of the world is at stake.

Conclusion

Christianity and Economics: Connections and Continued Progress

John Pisciotta

The previous essays are the outgrowth of the Baylor Christianity and Economics Conference around three themes: (1) Economist as Mainstream Scholar, (2) Economist as Policy Advocate, and (3) Economist as Philosopher. George M. Marsden sets the table with his framework for Christian scholarship in the academy. Judith M. Dean offers the perspective of the mainstream scholar. The policy advocates are Rebecca M. Blank and Glenn C. Loury. The philosophical (even theological) views come from Michael Novak, Robert H. Nelson, and David P. Gushee.

This concluding chapter looks back at chapters two through eight to make connections between the chapters and the themes of the conference. This chapter also reflects on prospects for further progress in Christian scholarship in economics. In the attempt to draw connections, some key points of the authors are highlighted. In addition to the perspectives of the author, this concluding chapter also utilizes comments from the closing panel discussion of the conference.

The four panelists were Kenneth G. Elzinga of the University of Virginia, James P. Tiemstra of Calvin College, Andrew M. Yuengert of Pepperdine University, and Earl L. Grinols of the University of Illinois, at the time of the conference. All the panelists were economists.

Regarding scholarship of the three varieties, it is implicit that few scholars will be active and effective in all three areas. As Judith Dean points out, individual scholars will specialize in different areas of the Christian-scholarship vineyard. It will be tempting for individual scholars to see their way as the best way. For a robust Christian influence on scholarship in economics, it is more helpful to see scholarship connections—whether complementary or in conflict.

THE OUTRAGEOUS IDEA

With his prodigious scholarship as a historian and with the publication of *The Outrageous Idea of Christian Scholarship* in 1997, George Marsden has provided a model in his discipline and encouragement for Christian scholarship in other disciplines. The Christianity and Economics Conference itself was evidence of success in the Marsden venture. For Christian scholarship, Marsden points to the influence of background belief, selection of research agenda, and ways of interpreting research data. All these influences were well represented in the conference.

While George Marsden noted the problem of "trivialization of Christianity" in the twentieth century, closing panelist Earl Grinols pointed to hopeful signs for the twenty-first century. Among the signs of growing respect for and openness to Christianity and religion in general are President Bush's faith-based initiative for antipoverty programs and Senator Joseph Lieberman's openness about his Jewish faith as a vice-presidential candidate in 2000. The increased openness to religion is in part a response to failure of past paradigms. For example, President Bush's faith-based initiative comes at a time when secular policies for the reduction of poverty have brought disappointing results.

Earl Grinols also emphasized that the handicap of Christian scholarship in the academy may be in part self-imposed. Grinols compared Christians in the academy to the Ents, the tree beings in J.R.R. Tolkien's *The Lord of the Rings.* The Ents were deeply rooted but largely passive for decade after decade. But when the Ents were awakened and challenged, they realized they were very strong and capable of taking action. Christians in the academy may be comparable to Tolkien's Ents—weak, at least in part, because they have regarded themselves as weak.

THE MAINSTREAM SCHOLAR

Judith Dean makes a spirited defense for the involvement of Christian economists in scholarship at the highest levels of the mainstream of the discipline. She writes, "It takes quality scholarship, as defined by the mainstream, to get a seat at the discussion table" (above, p. 25). As she explains, mainstream scholarship by Christian economists will not overtly reveal a Christian foundation or perspective. However, Dean believes that her own research in international trade, and the research of other Christian scholars, can be influenced by Christianity in the choice of research topics, the formulation of research questions, and the way the implication of research is evaluated. Topics that should be of special interest to Christian economists include stewardship of the earth, health care, poverty, debt, and debt forgiveness.

The metaphor Dean offers for the mainstream scholar is "research physician" for the economic system. There are economic diseases out there. As a research physician, the mainstream scholar does not engage in philosophical discussions of diseases, nor does he engage in the application of economic policies. What the research physician does is develop sound and relevant knowledge that practicing physicians can use to combat economic diseases.

The mainstream scholar approach is the most accessible application of Christian faith to professional life. Economists are graduates of major research universities with training in mainstream theoretical and statistical techniques. As they enter their careers as economists, the tool kit they have available is most productive for application in mainstream research. While Dean does not mention this factor, if an economist's career begins at a college or university, tenure pressures economists to stay within a mainstream research agenda. Such tenure pressures or incentives are prevalent in Christian as well as secular colleges and universities.

Dean by no means looks down on the work of policy advocates and economic philosophers. What she suggests is there may be a progression for some economists, from mainstream scholar to policy advocate and eventually to economic philosopher. In this transition, the economist may maintain former interests. A more senior economist working on matters of economic philosophy could still be involved in policy issues and mainstream research.

While Dean was forbearing to the economic philosophers, the economic philosophers did not fully return the favor. At many points in the conference, there were challenges to the validity of mainstream research, particularly to the extent that it relies on neoclassical models with the utility-maximizing, rational actor at center stage.

In chapter 7, Robert Nelson is highly critical of mainstream economics for claiming scientific objectivity while implicitly espousing a progressive "religion" of ever-expanding, earthly material welfare. Closing panelists Earl Grinols and Kenneth Elzinga expressed no reservations about Christian engagement in mainstream research. Both have had distinguished careers in mainstream research. However, John Tiemstra and Andrew Yuengert offered reservations about what could be achieved within the dominant paradigm of mainstream research. Tiemstra expressed concern that more realistic mainstream research does not filter through to policy formulation and instruction in economics classrooms. Moreover, neoclassical scholarship implies a strong determinism that he believes proscribes the impact of individual actions in the economy. For Yuengert, the big problem with the mainstream of economics is the focus on a narrow formulation of Homo Economicus, rather than a fuller and more realistic view of Homo Sapiens. We will return to economic philosophy shortly.

THE ECONOMIC POLICY ADVOCATE

Rebecca Blank and Glenn Loury present perspectives of policy advocates. While both address the application of economics, they have notable differences regarding their Christian experiences. Blank is a "cradle Christian." Loury came to Christian faith as an adult—after he was well along in his career as an economist. Blank focuses broadly on the economic process and its relationship to Christianity. Loury focuses more narrowly on race, poverty, and economic justice.

Coming from different backgrounds and policy interests, Blank and Loury also reveal some striking similarities. Both express reservations about the neoclassical model on matters such as self-interest, rational choice, incentives, and efficiency. But neither suggests starting anew from some other foundation. As policy advocates, they encourage humility for economists working within the mainstream of the discipline. What the mainstream has to offer is highly valuable. But economists should avoid the sins of pride and arrogance. What Christianity has to offer the discipline of economics is an important "value added." Looking through the neoclassical set of eye glasses can sharpen one's vision. Still, views of the world will be significantly limited without the vision provided by looking at the world and people's lives from a Christian perspective.

Blank notes that the temptation for the economist to view the world as capable of being explained through the economic way of thinking is prevalent in the first year of graduate study. The economist-in-formation is immersed in economic theory. Blank writes, "They live, eat, think, and breathe economics, spending long nights working on complex problems in economic theory" (above, p. 35). The purpose of such study is to teach the student to think like an economist. The typical result goes further. The first year graduate student comes away from the experience thinking *only* as an economist. Blank's life as a Christian helped protect her as a graduate student from falling into a myopic view of the world. She credits years of Sunday school and a heavy dose of social action involvement.

From the beginning of her career, the economic model of behaviors was viewed as "at best a partial view of the world" (above, p. 36). Still this partial view has much to offer for understanding the economic process and for formulating public policy. The competitive-market process fosters creativity, efficiency, and decentralization of power. But economists should be fully aware that the competitive model assumes the key actor in the economic process is the individual, that individuals are motivated by self-interest, and that the economic process improves when individuals have more rather than less in material terms.

The economic models of the economics profession do have strong predictive power and have gained widespread respect in the public square. This has provided additional temptation to pride rather than humility. Economists have responded to their success in analyzing the economic process by extending their models more broadly—giving market or cost–benefit analyses of marriage and politics. At the heart of these efforts is individualistic calculation of self-interest in term of costs and benefits.

Blank sees a significant clash between the economist's way of analyzing social interactions and the "widely held Christian messages about what constitutes 'right action'" (above, p. 41). In contrast to individualism, Christians are called to a life in community. Rather than self-interest, the Christian should be motivated by "other-interest." Scripture warns that material abundance can undermine discipleship. On the matter of choice, what people in fact choose as Christians is more important that simply having an ever-broadening range of choice.

Application of Biblical principles to economic policy and living in the modern-day economy does not lead Blank to reject the insights of mainstream economics. Indeed, understanding the economic model can be helpful for Christian economic engagement. An understanding of the market process with increasingly global dimensions makes it clear that other-interest involvements cannot be carried in all economic interactions. Markets, particularly worldwide markets, are inherently impersonal. People do not have a personal engagement with producers of the bananas they eat for breakfast. Realistically, other-interest involvement will largely be with those people who meet face-to-face—in families, communities, churches, and other organizations. Broader other-interest actions will often be mediated through voluntary organizations and the actions of governments.

Blank hopes churches and religious organizations will help with Biblical living in today's global market economy. Religious organizations can be pathways for individual Christian involvement in national and international ministries. And, church congregations can teach and become forums for exploration of effective discipleship in an economy dominated by free-market institutions.

Like Blank, Glenn Loury believes mainstream economists claim too much for the atomistic or individualistic approach to economic or social analysis. While Blank emphasizes the normative limitations, Loury also points to the inadequacies for analysis of race and poverty in the United States. Loury's Christian conversion came after years of scholarship as a mainstream economist. His conversion resulted in a profound change in the way he approached economics. He began to view economics and the problem of racial inequality in "relational" terms rather than in the "transactional" terms of neoclassical economics.

The orthodox transactional perspective is the outgrowth of viewing society as a collection of individuals. Societal interactions are the results of self-interested actions of autonomous individuals. Loury cites Gary Becker's *Economics of Discrimination* (1971) as an example of a transactional analysis of race. Becker provided deductive explanations of many racial disparities in society as implications of individual "taste for discrimination" (above, p. 56).

With his newfound Christian emphasis on community and mutual responsibility, Loury saw important shortcomings in the transactional approach. Christian faith gave Loury a different set of eye glasses to view the economy.

Loury notes that with a transactional emphasis on efficiency, racial profiling in law enforcement may seem like a good idea. From a relational approach, emphasizing who Christians are as community, Loury reaches a different conclusion. With racial profiling, Loury asserts, "pursuit of efficiency through profiling has the effect of sundering the community and debasing its values" (above, p. 52).

What Loury offers from his Christian suppositions is a broader, more dynamic way to view the reality of racial disparities and the policy paths out of racial dilemmas. He finds that racial inequality is so stubbornly persistent in America because of the problem of "biased social cognition." Note that the cognition is social, not individual. Loury's starting point for analysis is not individual action but social interaction.

Biased social cognition gives Loury a way to explain that racial disparities may be endogenous within social interactions rather than exogenously determined by firmly established biological or cultural characteristics. He illustrates with an example of mortgage and commercial loans in Black neighborhoods. Such loans may be in fact quite risky for the lender. But why? The answer may not be hardwired characteristics of Blacks. Rather, for various historical and cultural reasons, White neighbors and bank lenders may come to expect poor loan performance in Black neighborhoods. This may lead a number of lenders to tighten credit and a portion of Whites to move out of the neighborhood when a few Blacks move in. Property values fall. With lower property values, more Blacks move into the neighborhood. These new entrants to the neighborhood will have lower economic standing and weaker credit worthiness. The end result of self-fulfilling prophecies confirms the generalization that loans within Black neighborhoods are high risk.

This type of social dynamic is not the result of firmly ingrained social traits among Blacks. Nor is it the result of a deeply entrenched White racism. Yet biased social cognition nevertheless promotes racial disparity. Moreover, in view of the racial history of the United States, Christians and others should be drawn to initiatives to right racial injustice.

When Loury approaches public policy, he continues with a relational rather than transactional perspective. Reparations for Blacks are rejected because they are a transactional solution rather than a true community response to racial difficulties. A transactional perspective would hold that Whites have done $X amount of harm to Blacks. Now it is time for Whites to pay back the $X. From a Christian perceptive of love and mutual responsibility within community, Loury finds reparations wanting. If the reparations were paid, the quid pro quo obligation would be met. The public policy issue of race would then be closed.

The relational approach to public policy for racial justice would be far different from reparations. With an appreciation of biased social cognition, people should recognize that "durable racial inequality can be best understood as the outgrowth of a series of 'vicious circles of cumulative causation'" (above, p. 66). Without recrimination, race-baiting, and the abandonment of social responsibility, society would acknowledge its long history of racial disparity. There would be long-term commitments to work out current predicaments and move toward greater social justice in race relations. The solution would not be so simple as to establish a color-blind society. Color blindness is another type of transactional solution. The current U.S. racial divide is now enmeshed in numerous circles of biased social cognition. In order to tackle the problem of racial disparity, these circles must be correctly understood as a foundation for effective public policy.

Loury provides a model of scholarship explicitly influenced by Christian sensibilities leading to a theoretical perspective of relational social dynamics and biased social cognition. This perspective may not be uniquely dependent on a Christian worldview. However, Loury's embrace of Christianity is what brings the "value added" to his analysis of race.

Loury elaborates on the implications of his relational analysis. He believes the relational perspective not only yields more accurate scientific analysis of race but also employs a fuller, more realistic view of the human person. This perspective goes beyond the materialist to the spiritual. Mainstream economics is effective in dealing with incentives and efficiency, but these matters are seen as of a "lower order than questions of spiritual identity" (above, p. 53). Cost–benefit calculus is important. Echoing Blank, Glenn Loury proclaims, "I am arguing against arrogance" (above, p. 54). Loury goes on to say, "Economics cannot finally resolve the most profound questions at the center of people's struggles as individuals, as families, and as a nation: Who are we? What must we do? How shall we live? What is right?" (above, p. 54).

The more narrow approach to the human person of the neoclassical model is necessarily focused on the material, the mechanistic, and a deterministic view of social interactions. The relational perspective, without such rigid determinism is more open to the positive interventions of individuals, families, organizations, and government policy.

In the closing panel, John Tiemstra applauded Loury regarding the deterministic bent of the neoclassical model. Tiemstra illustrated the deterministic problem of mainstream economics with the William Baumol and Alan Blinder principles of economics text that have been used at Calvin College. The text offered six themes to remember after the final exam. One of the six was, "The market will always get you." The authors meant that the market process provides determined results. And those who attempt to stray from market results—whether individuals or governmental decision-makers—will suffer for their transgressions.

Also in the closing panel, Earl Grinols shared his policy-advocate perspective that has resulted from his recent research transition toward the study of health care. Grinols called it a "framework for how things get done in society." He presented a five-fold classification of "agents for social action." The first is the purposeful action of individuals. Second, he spoke of the actions of voluntary groups of individuals, which today are often called NGOs or nongovernmental organizations. The third social actor is the decentralized operation of the market system. With a foundation of transactions between willing parties, the market system is voluntary in character. The fourth actor is government (or governments in a federal system), which can enforce actions and responses on a population. The fifth is the intervention of God in human affairs and events. While Christians acknowledge the latter, this is something they will not be able to address much in the scholarly arena.

Grinols urged Christian scholars to give strong consideration to what might be called "a good recipe" of ingredients of the five forces, to help build a society with greater flourishing of the Golden Rule and the second great commandment. Grinols observed that conference presentations and discussions generally gave greatest weight to actions of individuals and actions of governments, as compared to actions of voluntary organizations and markets. He called this a troubling imbalance in view of the coercive nature of government actions.

PHILOSOPHER OF ECONOMICS

Michael Novak, Robert H. Nelson, and David P. Gushee provide the economic philosophy chapters in this volume. The perspectives of Novak and Nelson are the outgrowth of intellectual conversion experiences in their lives. Gushee offers conclusions of years of Biblical scholarship.

These three chapters are difficult to connect. Like the conference from which these chapters originated, the breadth of perspectives is immense. Nelson began his career on the path of a mainstream scholar and soon became disillusioned. As a philosopher and theologian, Novak began with attachments to collective direction of the economy and was then drawn to capitalism. Gushee focuses primarily on what the Bible—both the Old and New Testaments—can tell or warn about the temptations permeating the economic dimensions of people's lives.

The three chapters can be considered with regard to two questions. First, how should one assess the value of the neoclassical model which dominates contemporary scholarship? Second, how should one assess the value of the capitalist economic process and the impact of this process on people's personal lives? Nelson is the major focus for the first question. Novak and Gushee will be compared for the second.

Coming from a family that placed a high value on scholarship, and entering Princeton University for graduate study in economics, Robert Nelson seemed destined to make his mark as an outstanding scholar within neoclassical economics. This career trajectory was not to be. Nelson increasingly stepped outside the neoclassical model to evaluate it as an "economic theologian." This is the title he gives to his body of critical analysis of economics. What Nelson saw in neoclassical economics was presuppositions of religious character. And the religion was by no means Christianity.

Nelson bluntly states the conclusion of years of theological reflection on his discipline: "Any economist, whether Christian or non-Christian, who actively participates in the current American economics profession is helping to advance the further marginalization of Christianity" (above, p. 90). He supports this conclusion with arguments that mainstream economics has its own teleology or account of the purpose of human life on earth, and its own account of good and evil.

The economics profession presents itself as a value-free science. Nelson rejects such an assessment. While the normative foundations of modern economics may be implicit, they are also deeply rooted. For the orthodox Christian, purpose on earth is to know, accept, and serve God with the expectation of being with him in eternity. In sharp contrast, the teleology of neoclassical economics is attaining "heaven on earth." The heaven people are promised, individually and as a society, is a heaven of material abundance. Relying on the engine of the market economy, supplemented by public policy relying on the wise counsel of the economics profession, material progress is possible and to be embraced by humanity. This affirms one of the perspectives of neoclassical economics mentioned in the chapter by Rebecca Blank: "more is always better" in the material sense. And, as far as the heart of neoclassical economics is concerned, the material sense is the only sense that matters.

As a corollary to the teleology Nelson finds in economics, he also points to its account of good and evil. Evil (or bad behaviorism) is the result of material deprivation. Evil can be expected to recede with material progress in society. This point of view is frequently presented in today's commentary regarding international terrorism. A common theme is that if the evil of terrorism is to subside, then there must be substantial material progress within the areas of the world where terrorism is nurtured.

Although not a professing Christian, Nelson rejects the "progressive" teleology of neoclassical economics and is not persuaded by the account of good and evil. The experiences of the U.S. War on Poverty and the tragedy of September 11, 2001 do not correspond to the progressive materialistic account of bad behavior in society.

Many Christians today are concerned about the power of secularizing forces in contemporary society. The commonly held view is that secularism—and the marginalization of Judeo-Christian religion—is far advanced in Europe. America has not been immune to the forces of secularization. Nelson provocatively argues that the scholarship and teaching (preaching?) of neoclassical economics is one of the secularizing forces in our society. Nelson writes, "The economics profession is itself the priesthood of a powerful secular religion" (above, p. 90).

In the closing conference panel, John Tiemstra joined Nelson in offering the critique of neoclassical economics. Tiemstra's views were briefly mentioned in the previous sections on "The Mainstream Scholar" and "The Economic Policy Advocate." According to Tiemstra, a key defense of the neoclassical paradigm is that the simple model has been elaborated in recent years to include imperfect competition, limited information, altruism, and other real-world factors. While Tiemstra applauds those working on neoclassical elaborations of the basic model, this does not set aside his misgivings. The simple neoclassical model is still the foundation for most discussion of public policy. Likewise, it is the simple neoclassical model that permeates college instruction in economics. The more realistic facets of the model just do not filter down to the crucial areas of policy making and education of today's students.

Tiemstra's greatest problem with the neoclassical model is its "determinism." While appreciating the market system benefits that are explained by neoclassical economics, Tiemstra proposes that Christians—as individuals, business managers, and government policy-makers—can elude the deterministic confinement of the market box. While market forces constrain actions, wide latitude for creative change still remains. If Christians believe that specific market results are rigidly determined, they will be blind to the existing opportunities for positive personal and governmental actions. And, those opportunities need not focus on the materialistic values that Nelson believes are at the center of neoclassical economics.

Now let me consider the second philosophical question. How do people assess the value of the capitalist economic process and the impact of this process on their personal lives? First, I will consider theologian Michael Novak. Novak evolved from a sympathetic view of collective control of the economy to affirming market capitalism as the preferred way to organize contemporary economies.

Kenneth Elzinga, in the closing panel, raised an interesting point relating Novak's conversion to neoclassical scholarship. Elzinga found it troubling that Novak came to appreciate market capitalism by reading the work of sociologists. To Elzinga, this is like finding out that a person "came to faith in Christ by reading *Das Capital*."

Novak's intellectual journey should give pause to neoclassical economists regarding their own scholarship and teaching. Could it be that some sociologists, and their pupils like Novak, are better teachers of the benefits of markets than economists writing and teaching within the neoclassical framework? Novak credits the influence of sociologists Peter Berger and Sidney Hook, who had previously taken the intellectual journey from advocacy of collectivism to support of capitalism. The economists Novak credits in his conversion story are F. A. Hayek and Ludwig von Mises. Hayek and Mises were leaders of the heterodox Austrian School of economics—with work far out of the economics mainstream. Elzinga questioned whether the content of contemporary economics courses, relying on the neoclassical model, conveys the dynamics of markets and the ennobling spirit of enterprise.

As a graduate student in theology, Novak "was instructed by Paul Tillich at Harvard (and not by him alone), that a Christian theologian *must* be a socialist" (above, p. 75). This was Novak's formative position regarding the grand choice between socialism and capitalism. Rather than "going with the dominant flow" of theology, philosophy, and the humanities, Novak decided to pursue his own study of economic systems. While Harvard mentors taught that capitalism was immoral, Novak entertained the thought that capitalism might be amoral. He hardly imagined that he would one day come to the conclusion that capitalism and its entrepreneurial leaders are a positive moral force in society.

Novak does not downplay his transformation, stating at the outset of his chapter, "Business is a noble Christian vocation, a work of social justice, and the single greatest institutional hope of the poor of the world, if the poor are to move up and out of poverty" (above, p. 73). A key insight that would lead Novak to this conclusion is that collectivists—whether of the Left or the Right—compare the imperfect reality of capitalism to an imagined, often utopian, world of socialism. Seeing such a comparison as invalid, Novak followed Aristotle's advice to study real-world specimens.

The study of the specimens of capitalism and socialism led eventually to the publication of *The Spirit of Democratic Capitalism* in 1982. Novak reached the conclusion that on economic, political and cultural grounds, capitalism combined with limited government in a democracy is the superior political–economic option for contemporary societies. Briefly, on the economic front, capitalism unleashes the initiatives and creativity for entrepreneurs and workers to combat the oppressive poverty that is prevalent in many nations. Politically, capitalism with limited government fosters personal freedom and freedom of association worthy of the dignity of the human person. Culturally, democratic capitalism views the mediating institution of family, church, and a myriad of other associations as valuable for a healthy society. In a socialist political economy, mediating institutions are typically regarded as a threat to stability, control, and purposes of the state.

In contemporary intellectual life, something that troubles Novak is the continued disdain or low regard for capitalism and business entrepreneurs on the part of religious and theological leaders. This attitude continued even after the 1989–1991 fall of Communist socialism. Toward the end of Novak's chapter, he takes to task the views expressed by Joerg Rieger of the Perkins School of Theology at Southern Methodist University. Novak is correct in challenging Rieger's view that capitalism per se diminishes the economic standing of working people. But is Novak's defense of capitalism too broad? Rieger is dismayed over the cultural impact of pervasive advertising in modern capitalism. Novak responds that businesses frequently fail in efforts to mold consumer behavior to promote their products. While Novak may be correct, Rieger's point is that the cumulative effect of advertising may turn Christians away from discipleship in building the kingdom of God.

Radical discipleship to work for the kingdom of God is the focus of the chapter by David P. Gushee. The essays by Novak and Gushee are in a sense very far apart. While both would call themselves theologians, their areas of investigation are quite distinct. From his theological background, Novak is drawn to the study of economic systems. Gushee gives us a detailed survey of the Bible and of fellow theologians to inquire into the economic ethics of Jesus Christ.

The body of what Gushee writes contains no explicit endorsement or criticism of capitalism. However, one could easily read into Gushee's writing an implicit criticism of capitalism. Gushee may be one of the theologians that perplex Novak. The following paragraph is a succinct summary of Gushee's conclusions:

> Seeing the inbreaking reign of God when most do not, the follower of Jesus is overjoyed at the opportunity to participate in the kingdom's dynamic advance in every area, economic life included. Living simply, not hoarding wealth, and trusting God to meet basic material needs are practices that free people to offer generosity to and seek justice for and with the poor and hungry and, in general, to follow Jesus. Finally, in turning hearts and eyes in this direction they themselves enjoy the added benefit of a remarkable personal liberation that yanks them free from greed, acquisitiveness, and a fruitless worry over treasures that will all too soon pass away. (above, p. 124)

Novak's purpose and Gushee's purpose are far apart but not necessarily contradictory. Novak tries to determine what economic system, between the two major competitors, would be preferred from a Christian perspective. Gushee offers Christian advice for discipleship that could apply to life in any economics system. Since Americans live in a predominantly capitalist system, one can assume the advice is primarily meant for those living in capitalist economies. The admonitions are many, addressing the danger of material possessions, greed, luxury, and hoarding. The conclusions of Novak and Gushee are of great interest for consideration of Christianity and economics. However, their conclusions do not substantially engage each other.

CONCLUSION

The chapters in this volume reflect the great range of scholarship of the 2002 Christianity and Economics Conference. This concluding essay has tried to draw connections between the works of the major contributors of the conference. Yet works of each author remain at some distance. Many additional roads and bridges are needed to further develop Marsden's outrageous idea of Christian scholarship in the discipline of economics. Closing panelists John Tiemstra and Andrew Yuengert offered suggestions for advancing this scholarship.

Tiemstra noted that policy discussion in areas such as health care, poverty, taxation, energy, and the environment was not prominent in the conference. The reason, according to Tiemstra, is that Christians within various traditions are deeply divided on these issues. They are embarrassed by their large divisions and therefore tend to avoid the issues. Remarkably, Christians seem to be able to handle their theological differences better than their economic-policy divisions. Tiemstra urges Christians in the academy to set aside their embarrassment and apprehension and engage one another on economic-policy issues. He offers suggestions on how to do this.

First, each Christian should conduct a personal evaluation to ask if his or her fundamental commitment is to Christianity or to some political ideology. If one finds her policy positions always line up with either the Republican or Democratic parties, this could be a hint that further self-evaluation could be useful. Glenn Loury is viewed as a good role model. Loury's policy positions of recent years reveal an unpredictability that upsets some people. Possibly, the Left and the Right are disconcerted with Glenn Loury because he is putting his Christian commitment before politics.

The second necessary element for fruitful discussion among Christians on public policy is to take the arguments of opponents seriously. Christians should not be too quick to dismiss the arguments of opponents as self-serving or based on bad economics. They should work hard to understand just where and how they disagree with colleagues.

Andrew Yuengert asked the important question, "What should we do differently as a result of the conference we have just experienced?" Christian economists should not determine what they should do differently by acting as the Homo Economicus of their economic models. Rather, they should approach this question as real Homo Sapiens of the Christian persuasion.

Economists have a special problem in answering: "What should I do?" This is because they are overly influenced by the model of individual decision-making. As Homo Economicus, each would perform a cost-benefit recalculation with regard to scholarship agenda. In particular, they would reflect on whether personal preferences have changed and whether external incentives have changed. As a result of the conference, participants' "tastes" for explicitly Christian scholarship may have changed. Regarding incentives, one may have discovered a new source of funding for a Christian research project. Or, one might have come to realize that Christian scholarship is more respected in the academy and possibly in one's institution. After a full reflection on preferences and incentives, Homo Economicus would then do a rational recalculation that might lead to more research with Christian content.

Yuengert counsels against this approach and argues that it involves a misunderstanding of the role of the created Homo Economicus. The simplified view of man was developed as a model useful in theory and prediction of aggregate human behavior. The Homo Economicus model does not require or advocate that any particular person actually behave in this manner.

As Homo Sapiens, Christian economists will make decisions about scholarship by delving far beyond a reflection on preferences and incentives. In particular, they will consciously think about "the reasons" for engaging in future research projects. They will ask: Why am I using my time to do this? What is the good that will come from this effort? Should I do this in light of my understanding of the gospel? Does this project really contribute to my vocation as a scholar?

In *The Outrageous Idea of Christian Scholarship,* George Marsden issued a challenge and call to action to Christians regarding scholarship. Earl Grinols reminded us of Tolkien's Ents. Like the Ents, let Christian scholars realize that they have much more capacity for discipleship in vocations in economics than they may have been aware of in the past.

Bibliography

Allison, Dale C. (1989). *The Sermon on the Mount: Inspiring the moral imagination.* New York: Herder & Herder.

Arrow, Kenneth J. (1983). *Collected papers: Vol. 1. Social choice and justice.* Cambridge, MA: MIT Press.

Becker, Gary S. (1971). *The economics of discrimination* (2nd ed.). Chicago: University of Chicago Press.

Berger, Peter. (1974). *Pyramids of sacrifice.* New York: Basic Books.

———. (Ed.). (1986). *The capitalist revolution: Fifty propositions about prosperity, equality, and liberty.* New York: Basic Books.

———. (Ed.). (1987). *Capitalism and equality in America.* New York: Institute for Economics Affairs.

———. (1987). *Capitalism and equality in Third World.* New York: Institute for Economics Affairs.

Berry, Wendell. (1987). *Home economics.* San Francisco: North Press.

Betz, Hans Dieter. (1995). *The Sermon on the Mount.* Minneapolis: Fortress.

Blank, Rebecca M. (1997). *It takes a nation.* Princeton, NJ: Princeton University Press.

Blank, Rebecca M. & William McGurn. (2003). *Is the market moral? A dialogue on religion, economics, and justice.* Washington, DC: Brookings Institution Press.

Boaz, David. (1997). *Libertarianism: A primer.* New York: Free Press.

Bockmuehl, Markus. (1994). *This Jesus: Martyr, Lord, Messiah.* Downers Grove, IL: InterVarsity Press.

Bonhoeffer, Dietrich. (1995). *The cost of discipleship.* New York: Simon & Schuster.

Borg, Marcus. (1998). *Conflict, holiness, and politics in the teachings of Jesus.* Harrisburg, PA: Trinity Press.

Boulding, Kenneth E. (1968). *Beyond economics: Essays on society, religion, and ethics.* Ann Arbor: University of Michigan Press.

Bourdieu, Pierre. (1998, December). The essence of neoliberalism: Utopia of endless exploitation [English ed., electronic version]. *Le monde diplomatique* (Jeremy J. Shapiro, Trans.).

Carter, Stephen L. (1993). *The culture of disbelief: How American law and politics trivialize religious devotion.* New York: Basic Books.

Chapman, Colin A., Wrangham, Richard, & Chapman, Lauren J. (1995). Ecological constraints on group size: An analysis of spider monkey and chimpanzee subgroups. *Behavioral Ecology and Sociobiology, 36,* 59–70.

Cone, James H. (1997). *God of the oppressed,* Maryknoll, NY: Orbis Books.

Crossan, John Dominic. (1996). *Who killed jesus? Exposing the roots of anti-Semitism in the Gospel story of the death of Jesus.* San Francisco: Harper.

Davies, W. D., "Ethics in the New Testament," In George Buttrick (Ed.), *The Interpreter's Dictionary of the Bible. Vol 2.* New York: Abingdon Press.

———. (1964). *The setting of the Sermon on the Mount.* Cambridge: Cambridge University Press.

Davies, W. D. & Allison, Dale. (1988). *A critical and exegetical commentary on the Gospel according to St. Matthew: Voll. 1. Introduction and commentary on Matthew I–VII.* Edinburgh: T & T Clark.

Dean, Judith M. (1990). The effects of the U.S. MFA on small exporters. *Review of Economics and Statistics, 1,* 63–69.

———. (1992). Trade and the environment: A survey of the literature. In P. Low (Ed.), *International trade and the environment* (pp. 15–28). World Bank discussion paper, no. 159. Washington, DC: World Bank Publications.

———. (1995). Export bans, environment, and developing country welfare. *Review of International Economics, 3,* 319–29.

———. (1995). Market disruption and the incidence of VERs under the MFA. *Review of Economics and Statistics, 2,* 383–88.

———. (1999a). Testing the impact of trade liberalization on the environment: Theory and evidence. in P. Fredriksson (Ed.), *Trade, global policy, and the environment* (pp. 55–64). World Bank discussion paper, no. 402. Washington, DC: World Bank Publications.

———. (Ed.) (2001). *International trade and the environment.* The international library of environmental economics and policy. Aldershot, Hants, England: Ashgate.

———. (2002). Does trade liberalization harm the environment? A new test. *Canadian Journal of Economics, 35,* 819–42.

Dean, Judith M., & Gangopadhyay, S. (1991). Market equilibrium under the "threat" of a VER. *Journal of International Economics, 30,* 137–52.

———. (1992). Strategic trade practices in the presence of a VER. *International Economic Review, 33,* 645–59.

———. (1997). Export bans, environmental protection, and unemployment. *Review of Development Economics, 1,* 324–36.

Eberstadt, Nicholas. (2002, September 7). Population sense and nonsense. *The Weekly Standard,* pp. 29–33.

Evans, C. Stephen. (1999). Christian scholarship. *Christians and Scholarship, 2.*

Fee, Gordon D. (1992). The Kingdom of God. In Murray Dempster, Byron D. Klause, & Douglas Petersen (Eds.), *Called and empowered: Pentecostal perspectives on global mission.* Peabody, MA: Hendrickson.

Frank, Robert H., Gilovich, Thomas D., & Regan, Dennis T. (1996). Do economists make bad citizens? *Journal of Economic Perspectives, 10(1),* 187–92.

———. Gilovich, Thomas D., & Regan, Dennis T. (1993). Does studying economics inhibit cooperation? *Journal of Economic Perspectives, 7(2)*, 159–71.

Fredriksson, P. (Ed.). (1999). *Trade, global policy, and the environment.* World Bank discussion paper, no. 402. Washington, DC: World Bank Publications.

Friedman, Milton. (1953). The methodology of positive economics. In Milton Friedman (Ed.), *Essays in positive economics* (pp. 3–43). Chicago: University of Chicago Press.

———. (1962). *Capitalism and freedom.* Chicago: University of Chicago Press.

Garland, David E. (1996). *Mark: The NIV application commentary.* Grand Rapids, MI: Zondervan.

Green, Joel B. (1997). *The Gospel of Luke,* Grand Rapids, MI: Eerdmans.

Guelich, Robert. (1982). *The Sermon on the Mount: A foundation for understanding,* Waco, TX: Word.

Gundry, Robert H. (1994). *Matthew* (2nd ed.). Grand Rapids, MI: Eerdmans.

Hagner, Donald A. (1993). *Matthew 1–13.* Word Biblical commentary 33A. Waco, TX: Word.

Hampshire, Stuart, & Kolakowski, Leszek. (1974). *The socialist idea.* New York: Basic Books.

Harrington, Michael. (1968). *Toward a democratic left.* New York: Macmillan.

Harrison, Lawrence. (2000). *Culture matters: How values shape human progress.* New York: Basic Books.

Hausman, Daniel M., & McPherson, Michael S. (1996). *Economic analysis and moral philosophy.* New York: Cambridge University Press.

Hauwerwas, Stanley. (2001). *Christian existence today: Essays on church, world, and living in between.* Grand Rapids, MI: Brazos Press.

Hayek, F. A. (1971). *The intellectuals and socialism.* Menlo Park, CA: Institute for Humane Studies.

———. (1972). *The road to serfdom.* Chicago: University of Chicago Press.

Hays, Richard B. (1996). *The moral vision of the New Testament: Community, cross, new creation.* New York: HarperCollins.

Heilbroner, Robert. (1974). *An inquiry into the human prospect.* New York: W. W. Norton.

———. (1980). *Marxism: For and against.* New York: W. W. Norton.

Henderson, James W. (2005). *Health economics and policy* (3rd ed.). Mason, OH: Thomson South-Western.

Henderson, James W., & Pisciotta, John. (Eds.). (2003). [Special Issue]. *Journal of Markets & Morality, 6(2).*

Herzog, William II. (2000). *Jesus, justice, and the reign of God.* Louisville, KY: Westminster John Knox.

Hodgson, Godfrey. (2000). *The gentleman from New York: Daniel Patrick Moynihan.* Boston: Houghton Mifflin.

Hook, Sidney. (1974). *Pragmatism and the tragic sense of life.* New York: Basic Books.

Howe, Irving. (1979). Introduction. In Irving Howe (Ed.), *Twenty-five years of dissent: An American tradition.* New York: Methuen.

Hultgren, Arland J. (2002). *The parables of Jesus: A commentary.* Grand Rapids, MI: Eerdmans.

Institute for Educational Affairs and Roper Center. (1982). Theology faculty survey: The findings. *This World, 2,* 27–75.

Internal Revenue Service. Individual income tax returns with positive adjusted gross income (AGI): Number of returns, shares of AGI and total income tax, and average tax rates, by selected ascending cumulative percentiles of returns based on income size using the definition of AGI for each year, tax years 1986–2000. Retrieved October 29, 2002, from http://www/irs.gov/pub/irs-soi/00in02rt.xls

Johnson, Paul. (1977). *The enemies of society.* New York: Atheneum.

Kahneman, Daniel, & Tversky, Amos. (1979). Prospect theory: An analysis of decision under risk. *Econometrica, 47,* 263–92.

Keener, Craig S. (1993). *The IVP Bible background commentary: New Testament.* Downers Grove, IL: InterVarsity Press.

Keynes, John Maynard. (1965). *The general theory of employment, interest, and money* (1st Harbinger ed.). New York: Harcourt, Brace, & World.

Kolakowski, Leszek. (1978). *Main currents of Marxism: Its rise, growth, and dissolution: Vol. 3. Breakdown.* (P. S. Falla, Trans.). Oxford: Clarendon Press.

Koop, C. Everett, & Johnson, Timothy. (1992). *Let's talk: An honest conversation on critical issues: Abortion, euthanasia, AIDS, health care.* Grand Rapids, MI: Zondervan.

Kraybill, Donald B. (1978). *The upside-down kingdom.* Scottdale, PA: Herald Press.

Lahaye, Timothy, & Jenkins, Jerry B. (1996). *Left behind: A novel of the earth's last days.* Wheaton, IL: Tyndale House.

Lazear, Edward P. (2000). Economic imperialism. *Quarterly Journal of Economics, 115,* 99–146.

Loury, Glenn C. (2002). *The anatomy of racial inequality,* Cambridge, MA: Harvard University Press.

Low, P. (Ed.). (1992). *International trade and the environment.* World Bank discussion paper, no. 159. Washington, DC: World Bank Publications.

Machlup, Fritz. (1969). Positive and normative economics. In Robert Heilbroner (Ed.), *Economic means and social ends: Essays in political economics* (pp. 99–124). Englewood Cliffs, NJ: Prentice-Hall.

Maritain, Jacques. (1958). *Reflections on America.* Scribner.

Marsden, George M. (1994). *The soul of the American university: From Protestant establishment to established nonbelief.* New York: Oxford University Press.

———. (1997). *The outrageous idea of Christian scholarship.* New York: Oxford University Press.

———. (2002). Beyond progressive scientific humanism. In Paul J. Dovre (Ed.), *The future of religious colleges* (pp. 44–49). Grand Rapids, MI: Eerdmans.

Marx, Karl, & Engels, Friedrich. (1848). The Communist Manifesto. London.

———. (1959). *Manifesto on the Communist party.* In Lews S. Feuer (Ed.), *Basic writings on politics and philosophy* (pp. 1–41). Garden City, NY: Anchor Books.

Mayer, J.P. (Ed.). (1969). *Democracy in America* (George Lawrence, Trans.). New York: Anchor Books.

McCloskey, Donald N. (June 1983). The rhetoric of economics. *Journal of Economic Literature, 21,* 481–517.

Mises, Ludwig von. (1981). *Socialism: An economic and sociological analysis,* (J. Kahane, Trans.). Indianapolis: Liberty Classics.

Muir, John. (1968). *Gentle wilderness: The Sierra Nevade.* San Francisco: Ballentine Books.

Murray, Charles. (1997). *What it means to be a Libertarian: A personal interpretation.* New York: Broadway Books.

Myers, Ched. (1997). *Binding the strong man.* Maryknoll, NY: Orbis.

Nelson, Robert H. (1987). The Economics profession and the making of public policy. *Journal of Economic Literature, 25,* 49–91.

———. (1990). Unoriginal sin: The Judeo-Christian roots of ecotheology. *Policy Review, 53,* 52–59.

———. (1991). *Reaching for heaven on Earth: The theological meaning of economics.* Lanham, MD: Rowman & Littlefield.

———. (1993). Environmental Calvinism: The Judeo-Christian roots of environmental theology. In Roger E. Meiners & Bruce Yandle (Eds.), *Taking the environment seriously.* Lanham, MD.: Rowman & Littlefield, 233–55.

———. (1994). Economics as religion. In H. Geoffrey Brennan & A. M. C. Waterman (Eds.), *Economics and religion: Are they distinct?* (pp. 227–36). Boston: Kluwer Academic.

———. (1995). Sustainability, efficiency and God: Economic values and the sustainability debate. *Annual review of ecology and systematics 26*, 135–54.

———. (1996, June 24). Bruce Babbitt, pipeline to the Almighty. *The Weekly Standard*, 17–19.

———. (1997a). Calvinism minus God: Environmental restoration as a theological concept. In L. Anathea Brooks & Stacy D. VanDeever (Eds.), *Saving the seas: Values, scientists and international governance.* College Park: Maryland Sea Grant College, 87–105.

———. (1997b). Does "existence value" exist? An essay on religions, old and new. *The Independent Review, 1*, 499–522.

———. (1997c). Religion as taught in the public schools. *Forbes, 160(1)*, 69.

———. (1998a) Calvinism minus God. *Forbes, 162 (7)*, 143.

———. (1998b). Economic religion versus Christian values. *Journal of Markets and Morality, 1*, 142–57.

———. (2001a). *Economics as religion: From Samuelson to Chicago and beyond.* University Park: Penn State Press.

———. (2001b). Frank Knight and original sin. *The Independent Review, 6*, 5–26.

———. (2003). Environmental colonialism: "Saving" Africa from Africans. *The Independent Review, 8*, 65–86.

North, Charles M., & Gwin, Carl R. (2004). Religious freedom and the unintended consequences of state religion. *Southern Economic Journal, 71*, 103–17.

Novak, Michael. (1982). *The spirit of democratic capitalism.* New York: Simon & Schuster.

———. (1984). *Catholic social thought and liberal institutions: Freedom with justice.* San Francisco: Harper & Row.

———. (1985). *Will it liberate?: Questions about liberation theology.* New York: Paulist.

———. (1989). *Free persons and the common good.* Lanham, MD: Madison Books.

———. (1990). *This hemisphere of liberty: A philosophy of the Americas.* Washington, DC: AEI Press.

———. (1993). *The Catholic ethic and the spirit of capitalism.* New York: Free Press.

———. (1996). *Business as a calling: Work and the examined Life.* New York: Simon & Schuster.

———. (1996, January). Inequality and ideology. On the Issues. Retrieved June 20, 2005, from American Enterprise Institute Online, from http://www.aei.org/publications/pubID.6067/pub_detail.asp

———. (1997). *The fire of invention: Civil society and the future of the corporation.* Lanham, MD: Rowman & Littlefield.

———. (1999). *On cultivating liberty: Reflections on a moral ecology.* Lanham, MD: Rowman & Littlefield.

———. (2002, August 16). The moral heart of capitalism. *National review online.* Retrieved June 20, 2005, from http://www.nationalreview.com/novak/novak081602.asp

Opitz, Edmund A. (1999). *The libertarian theology of freedom.* Tampa, FL: Hallberg.

Pallares, Pedro. (2003, October). The poor as a person: Roots of the roads against poverty. Paper presented at the Formation and Renewal Conference at the University of Notre Dame, Notre Dame, IN.

Rieger, Joerg. (2002). Theology and economics. *Religious Studies Review, 28(3)*, 215–20.

Roberts, Paul Craig. (2002, October 23). Criminalizing business. *The Washington Times.*

Sanders, E.P. (1985). *Jesus and Judaism.* Philadelphia: Fortress.

Sauer, James. (2002, November). Christian faith, economy, and economics: What do Christian ethics contribute to understanding economies? Paper presented at the conference "Christianity and Economics: Integrating Faith and Learning in Economic Scholarship," hosted by the Lilly Fellows Program and Baylor University, Waco, TX.

Schelling, Thomas C. (1978). *Micromotives and macrobehavior.* New York: Norton.

Schumpeter, Joseph A. (1942). *Capitalism, socialism, and democracy.* New York: Harper.

Sen, Amartya. (1987). *On ethics & economics.* Oxford: Blackwell.

Shafarevich, Igor. (1980). *The socialist phenomenon.* (William Tjalsma, Trans.). New York: Harper & Row.

Smith, Adam. (1937). *An inquiry into the nature and causes of the wealth of nations* (Edwin Cannan, Ed.). New York: Random House.

———. (1975). *The theory of moral sentiments* (D. D. Raphael & A. L. Macfie, Eds.). Oxford: Clarendon Press.

Smith, Stephen L. S. & Webb, Bruce G. (Eds.). (2003). *Faith & Economics, 42.*

Smith, Vernon L. (2000). *Bargaining and market behavior: essays in experimental economics.* Cambridge, MA: Cambridge University Press.

Stamp, Josiah. (1926). *The Christian ethic as an economic factor.* London: Epworth Press.

———. (1939). *Christianity and economics.* New York: Macmillan.

Stassen, Glen H., & Gushee, David P. (2003). *Kingdom ethics: Following Jesus in contemporary context,* Downers Grove, IL: InterVarsity Press.

Thaler, Richard. (1980). Toward a positive theory of consumer choice. *Journal of Economic Behavior and Organization, 1,* 39–60.

Tocqueville, Alexis de. (1969). *Democracy in America.* (George Lawrence, Trans. & J. P. Mayer, Ed.). New York: Anchor Books.

Trocme, Andre. (1973). *Jesus and the nonviolent revolution.* Scottdale, PA: Herald Press.

United Church of Christ. (1989). General synod pronouncement on Christian faith, economic life, and justice. September 20, 2005, from http://www.ucc.org/justice/book/jw9.pdf

U.S. Catholic Bishops. (1986). Economic justice for all: Catholic social teaching and the U.S. economy. *Origins, 16(24),* 409–55.

U.S. International Trade Commission. (2002). *The economic effects of significant U.S. import restraints: Third update* (Investigation no. 332–325, Publication 3519). Washington, DC: U.S. Government Printing Office.

U.S. Small Business Administration. (2001). *Small business economic indicators, 2000.* Washington, DC: U.S. Government Printing Office.

Verhey, Allen. (1993). *The great reversal: Ethics and the New Testament.* Grand Rapids, MI: Eerdmans.

Vitz, Paul C. (1994). *Psychology as religion: The cult of self-worship.* Grand Rapids: Eerdmans.

Weber, Max. (1930). *The Protestant ethic and the spirit of capitalism.* New York: HarperCollins.

Wheaton College, Center for Applied Christian Ethics Retrieved. Jubilee 2000: Our Debt to the Debtors. June 20, 2005, from http://www.wheaton.edu/CACE/events/archives/evarc08.htm

Wheeler, Sondra. (1995). *Wealth as peril and obligation.* Grand Rapids, MI: Eerdmans.

Wilber, Charles K., & Hoksbergen, Roland. (October 1986). Ethical values and economic theory: A survey. *Religious Studies Review, 12,* 208–14.

Wolterstorff, Nicholas. (1984). *Reason within the bounds of religion.* Grand Rapids, MI: William B. Eerdmans.

World Trade Organization. (2001). Ministered declaration. Doha Ministerial Conference, Fourth session, WT/MIN(01)/DEC/1. September 20, 2005, from http://www.wto.org/english/thewto_e/minist_e/min01_e/mindecl_e.htm

Wright, N. T. (1996). *Jesus and the victory of God.* Minneapolis: Fortress.

Yoder, John Howard. (1994). *The politics of Jesus* (2nd ed.). Grand Rapids, MI: Eerdmans.

Younkins, Edward W. (Ed.). (2001). *Three in One: Essays on democratic capitalism.* Lanham, MD: Rowman & Littlefield.

Zinsmeister, Karl. (2002). The shame of America's one-party campuses. *The American Enterprise, 13,* 18–25.

List of Contributors

David P. Gushee is the Graves Associate Professor of Moral Philosophy and senior fellow of the Carl F. H. Henry Center for Christian Leadership at Union University. Dr. Gushee has served on the staff of Evangelicals for Social Action and the faculty of Southern Baptist Theological Seminary in Louisville, Kentucky. In addition to degrees from the College of William and Mary and the Southern Baptist Theological Seminary, Dr. Gushee has a asters degree and Ph.D. in philosophy from Union Theological Seminary. He was listed as one of 50 "up and coming" evangelical leaders under the age of 40 by Christianity Today magazine in 1996. Among his contributions include roles in drafting the historic 1995 Southern Baptist Convention resolution on racial reconciliation and an important 1996 statement on abortion. Dr. Gushee has published extensively on a variety of subjects related to Christian life and witness, especially in the areas of social ethics and public policy.

George M. Marsden is the Francis A. McAnaney Professor of History at Notre Dame. Professor Marsden has also taught at Duke University Divinity School, Calvin College, Trinity Evangelical Divinity School, and the University of California at Berkeley. After graduating from Haverford College, he earned his B.D. from Westminster Theological Seminary, followed by masters and doctoral degrees from Yale University. Professor Marsden's primary academic interests are the history of the interaction of Christianity and American culture. He has received a number of honors, including a fellowship from the National

Endowment for the Humanities and a Guggenheim fellowship. He was the president of the American Society of Church History in 1992 and has served on the editorial boards of *Christian Scholar's Review, The Reformed Journal,* and *Perspectives.*

Glenn C. Loury is University Professor, Professor of Economics, and Director of the Institute on Race and Social Division at Boston University. Professor Loury has also taught at Harvard, Northwestern, and the University of Michigan. He earned a B.A. in mathematics at Northwestern University and holds a Ph.D. in economics from the Massachusetts Institute of Technology. A distinguished academic economist, Professor Loury has made scholarly contributions to the fields of welfare economics, game theory, industrial organization, natural resource economics, and the economics of income distribution. He is a fellow of the American Academy of Arts and Sciences, a fellow of the Econometric Society, and was elected vice president of the American Economics Association for 1997. He is a frequent commentator on national radio and television, a much sought-after public speaker and an adviser on social issues to business and political leaders throughout the country.

James W. Henderson is the Ben H. Williams Professor in Economics at Baylor University. He completed his undergraduate degree in finance at the University of Houston, received his Ph.D. from Southern Methodist University, and has taught at Baylor since 1981. Dr. Henderson's research interests are focused on health care issues. His most recent book entitled *Health Economics and Policy,* published by South-Western, is now in its third edition. His current research includes an examination of the cost of health insurance mandates; several cost-effectiveness studies, including cervical cancer screening and treatment alternatives for low-back pain; and alternatives to patents in the pharmaceutical drug industry.

John L. Pisciotta is an Associate Professor of Economics in Baylor University's Hankamer School of Business. He received an undergraduate degree in economics from the University of Colorado and a Ph.D. from the University of Texas at Austin. Before joining the Baylor faculty, Pisciotta served on the economics department of Colorado State University at Pueblo. Prior to 1987, he was Associate Director of the Center for Private Enterprise at Baylor. His research interests include K–12 education reform and the economic role of government. He is a senior fellow with the Texas Public Policy Foundation. He is actively involved in the pro-life activities of the Catholic Diocese of Austin.

Judith M. Dean is an international economist at the U.S. International Trade Commission. Dr. Dean has also taught at Bowdoin College and the School of Advanced International Studies, Johns Hopkins University. She received her undergraduate degree from Gordon College and her M.A. and Ph.D. from Cornell University. She has served as a consultant with the World Bank and the Organization for Economic Cooperation and Development, and on two separate occasions was a visiting scholar with the Indian Statistical Institute in New Delhi, India. Dr. Dean's primary research interest is the impact of trade policy on the environment, particularly as it relates to developing countries. Dr. Dean is past president of the Association of Christian Economists.

Michael Novak is the George Frederick Jewett Scholar in Religion, Philosophy and Public Policy and also the Director of Social and Political Studies at the American Enterprise Institute for Public Policy Research in Washington, DC. In addition to his 15 honorary degrees, he has earned bachelors degrees from Stonehill College and the Gregorian University in Rome, Italy. He also holds a masters degree in history and philosophy of religion from Harvard University. He is the 1999 recipient of the Francis Boyer Award and the most recent recipient of the Gold Medal of the Pennsylvania Society.

Rebecca M. Blank is Dean of the Gerald R. Ford School of Public Policy, Henry Carter Adams Collegiate Professor of Public Policy, and Professor of Economics at the University of Michigan. She served as a member of President Clinton's Council of Economic Advisers from 1997–1999. Professor Blank's research has focused on the interaction between the macroeconomy, government antipoverty programs, and the behavior and well-being of low-income families. Her book, *It Takes A Nation: A New Agenda for Fighting Poverty*, published in 1997, won the Richard A. Lester Prize for the Outstanding Book in Labor Economics and Industrial Relations. Professor Blank chaired the commission that wrote the United Church of Christ's "A Pronouncement on Christian Faith: Economic Life and Justice," passed by the General Synod in 1989.

Robert H. Nelson is professor of environmental policy at the School of Public Affairs of the University of Maryland and senior fellow for environmental studies at the Competitive Enterprise Institute. He has also worked in the Office of Policy Analysis of the Interior Department; the Commission on Fair Market Value Policy for Federal Coal Leasing; the Senate Select Committee on Indian Affairs; and served on the President's Commission on Privatization. He is a nationally recognized authority on land and natural resource management and has published extensively in those areas. He holds a B.A. from Brandeis University and a Ph.D. in economics from Princeton University.